The Laughter and the Weeping

An Old China Hand Remembers

Dear Hugh:
    We hope you have a
Merry Christmas and a Happy
New year.
    Father Luke O'Reilly is an old
friend from Ireland. He stayed
with us two weeks, a month or two
ago and said Mass in our House
for two weeks. He is back in
Ireland at Navan again which is
a semi retirement home for
Columban Fathers.
        Love to you,
            Rita & Bill

the columba press

First edition, 1991, published by
THE COLUMBA PRESS
93 The Rise, Mount Merrion, Blackrock, Co Dublin, Ireland

Cover by Bill Bolger
Origination by The Columba Press
Printed in England by Billings & Sons Ltd, Worcester

ISBN: 1 85607 021 2

The author would like to thank Jim Coffey, Editor of *The Scottish Catholic Observer* for permission to use extracts and Jim Kirwan, Managing Director of The Richview Press, for permission to use excerpts from the author's contribution to *But not conquered* ... .

For help in producing this story, I thank all the Columbans who were with me in Nancheng and who read the manuscript and made helpful suggestions; Pat Reilly, lecturer in Glasgow University; Sr Pauline McAndrew, a Columban sister; and to my confreres Warren Kinne, Chris Baker and Gerry Kelly. My thanks also to the typisis, Frances O'Donnell and Margaret Moran in Glasgow and Sandra Garry in Navan.

By way of bibliography, I used the following books: *My Country and my people*, (Lin Yutang); *Religious Freedom in China*, (Sword of the Spirit); *Into China*, (Claude Roy); *One's Company*, (Peter Fleming); *Against All Hope*, (Armando Valladares); *The Apocalypse*, (Fr Martindale SJ); *A New Pentecost*, (Cardinal Suenens).

Contents

*To the Columban co-missionaries, whether clergy or laity,
in Ireland, America, Australia, New Zealand,
Scotland, England, Wales,
this book is dedicated with gratitude and affection.*

Foreword

Once upon a time, there was a parish priest called Fr Sigismund in a parish in Europe. It appears that his sermons were a talking point frequently amongst his parishioners. A priest from a neighbouring parish, overcome by curiosity, said to one of Father Sigismund's parishioners, 'What is so special about Sigismund's sermons?' The devout and God-fearing man replied, 'The thing about Sigismund's sermons is this: nobody knows where the sermons are going to start, nobody knows where the sermons are going to finish. Neither does Sigismund.'

My presumption is that Fr Sigismund had the body of his sermon, but that he was frantically searching for an attention catching beginning and an unforgettable end, and that he was experiencing considerable difficulty in finding either. I have the body of my story, just as he had the body of his sermon, but I am searching vainly for an arresting beginning and a happy ending.

The body of my story is about the persecution of the Catholic Church in Nancheng, China, from 1950, when it started, right up to the present, 1990. The sources of the story are the 'Omaha memoirs', which I was shanghaied into dictating in 1954. But what was I doing anyhow in Omaha at that particular time? After nearly seven years in China, and four under the communists, I was hospitalised in Colorado Springs, Colorado, for nine months. When I was discharged from hospital, it was decided that I should go on a period of convalescence to the Columban Headquarters in the United States in Omaha.

The warmth of the welcome and the grand hospitality had a therapeutic effect for me. I was only a few days there, when who comes in but Donal O'Mahony. Donal had been a missionary in our Diocese of Nancheng, but got ill and was sent to Shanghai for treatment. By the time the treatment was finished, the communists had taken over China and so he was appointed to the United States and was now editor of the 'Far East'. Donal informed me casually that the director of the American region, Pete McPartland, would like to have my China memoirs on paper. He talked a little about it and said, as a kind of after-thought when he was returning to his office, 'By the way, there will be a stenographer available tomorrow morning at my office and if you could be there at ten, we could make a start. A few hours in the morning and a few hours in the afternoon is all you should attempt. The stenographer is first class at shorthand.'

The stenographer was a charming American girl, Ann Murphy; she was not only excellent at shorthand, but also at typing. In six or seven weeks of April and part of May 1954, she had typed about 270 pages. In preparing for the dictation, I tried to follow the sequence of events as they occurred since my arrival in China, right to the end. Each evening I would jot down a few headings and then try to remember the detailed events, dates and even conversations that came under each particular heading.

All the same, memory is fallible and so I got Frank Whelan, who was in Nancheng during the persecution with me, and who in 1954 was manager of the General Office in Omaha, to check on dates and events and so forth. Donal O'Mahony also did some checking and he had a number of magazines and reference books and files and letters. Donal also edited part of the text. Then when the manuscript was sent to Ireland, Bishop Cleary, who had been our bishop in Nancheng, looked over it, as also did Joe Flynn, Seamus O'Reilly and Barney O'Neill.

The second source of the story is the twenty-four page letter we received from Fr Jim Yang, a Chinese priest and Vicar General of Nancheng Diocese, in 1980, four years after the death of Mao Tse Tung. It was written in English and told of the heroic witness given by our eight Chinese priests during the thirty years of persecution since we left China.

After I received a copy of Jim Yang's letter, I decided that we had a very inspiring, a very encouraging story and that I should share the good news with you who have been our faithful co-workers, co-missionaries, over the years.

By 1988, things had got much more relaxed in Red China and

Seamus O'Reilly who, with me, was among the last priests out of China in 1953, returned to that country and visited Nancheng. He spent two weeks in China and sent us a very comprehensive and encouraging report. That report, you could say, is the third source of the story.

The title I have decided to give the story is 'The Laughter and the Weeping'. Originally, I had thought of 'The Weeping and the Laughter', a line from Ernest Dowdson's poem, but then I discovered that a novelist, Noel Barber, has written a bestseller called 'The Weeping and the Laughter' and I felt you just could not have two bestsellers with the same title!

Persecutions can bring pain and distress and shock, and so it would be insensitive to lead you abruptly into a persecution situation from page one. So, like Fr Sigismund in his sermon, I must search for a beginning for my story which will innoculate you against future pain and distress and brace you for any eventuality. With this in view, I am inviting you to join seventeen Columbans and myself on a leisurely trip to China ....

PART I:

Getting to China

CHAPTER 1

More Comedy than Comfort

Robert Louis Stevenson assures us 'that to travel hopefully is a better thing than to arrive'. My seventeen Columban confreres and I travelled about ten thousand miles from Liverpool to Shanghai aboard the 'Empress of Australia' and we can assure you that the journey's end was miles better than the journey. We left Liverpool on the 22nd September 1946 and the journey took six weeks.

The voyage provided us with more comedy than comfort, but then the 'Empress of Australia' was a troop ship, not a luxury liner. Besides, we were living in that era of unabated austerity which came in the wake of World War II. With nearly two thousand on board, the boat seemed overcrowded. No amount of hopeful travelling could lend a little elbow room to a congested cabin or inject a little more nourishment into a wartime menu. The passengers were, for the most part, members of the British forces. There were also some diplomats, but most of the civilians on board seemed to be exporting something to China, either tobacco or ships or whatever. We Columban missionaries were exporting the Good News of Christianity, but we soon discovered that there were other missionaries on board exporting a slightly different brand of the same commodity. There were roughly thirty missionaries from a variety of Christian denominations in England and Scotland on board, and I should think about ten of them were ladies. Everybody referred to us Columbans as 'The Padres' and our clerical dress made us easily recognisable.

The sleeping accomodation was the high point of our discomfort. We were quartered in cabins in the hold of the ship beside the engine room, sixteen of us to a cabin. As there was no air conditioning, we sometimes woke up at night sweating profusely and wondering if we were not in a Turkish bath. The bunks were in three tiers. I was on a top-tier bunk and beneath me was an executive of a ship-building company, who was returning to Hong Kong. He was a dignified, cultured grey-haired man about 55 years of age. The ages of The Padres ranged from 25 to 30 so the ship-building executive was about 25 years older than we were. Still, the first time we met him on deck we got into conversation and became good friends. He warned us though that he was not R.C. himself but a staunch member of the Church of Scotland and a native of Glasgow. Everybody seemed to be staunch about something or other in those days.

Then there was the matter of getting permission to say daily Mass on board. Two of our missionaries asked the officer concerned if we could have a room for this purpose from 6.30 a.m. to about 8.00 a.m. each day. His reply took them by surprise; he said, in his upper-crust English accent, that he could see no earthly reason why we should have a service every day. When they told him that to us Catholics the Mass is infinitely precious, he replied that he was all for religion too, but for religion in moderation. He added that he was no fanatic and that quite frankly this business of a daily service seemed to him like creeping fanaticism – religion run wild. Later that evening, the officer changed his mind and informed the missionaries who had approached him earlier that he had decided to give us a room where we could say Mass each day. He let them know, though, that he was giving permission against his better judgement and only because another officer had persuaded him to do so and that, quite frankly, his personal opinion was the same as when he first refused them.

A few days out of Liverpool, the sea became very choppy and rough and most of us went down with seasickness. It has been observed that passengers are in a 'no-win' situation when there is a bad outbreak of sea sickness. If one's sea health is so robust that one escapes sickness, there is a danger that one may become intolerably conceited as one watches fellow passengers stumbling and staggering and fumbling at anything to which they can hold on (such as a rail or a wall) as they grope their way back to their bunks. On the other hand, if a passenger gets bad sea sickness, there is a danger that, after his recovery, he may get vain and indulge in unseemly boasting about the indescribable torments he has endured during his sickness. There was little danger that I should become conceited on account of my sea health because I got what I considered a most virulent dose of sea sickness.

Sure enough, after I recovered, I found myself boasting about the incredible ordeal I had come through. In my years as a fairly good listener, I have noticed that quality boasting is always low key and that only low key boasting can command credibility, so in a self-effacing manner, I started to boast on low C about my sea sickness to this mild-mannered confrere. He listened carefully and then gave such a heart-rending litany of his disorders when he was ill that I wondered if I had not been feigning sea sickness. At great length, he spoke of his dizziness, of his nausea, of his retching, of his inability to eat, of the way he staggered around the deck and of the long sleepless nights of desolation when he awaited the dawn. I felt completely and embarrassingly out-boasted as he recounted to me, in great detail, the list of his agonies. For the rest of that voyage, I kept quiet about my seasickness.

When we entered the Mediterranean we left seasickness behind us and we enjoyed sea health for the rest of the voyage. We left our black suits behind us too, or at least put them in moth balls and donned white tropical gear. Walking on the promenade deck was quite pleasant. The passengers we met there were friendly and we got to know a number of them. We met other passengers at the bridge tournament, which was one of the forms of recreation organised during the voyage. A large number of passengers played in the tournament. During our seminary days, our Easter vacation was always spent in the seminary, and we played bridge each night. It did not mean, of course, that we were all good players, but two of our missionaries did win a competition and the rest of us enjoyed the game very much indeed. However, some missionaries of other denominations were saddened and disappointed when they saw us playing; they said nothing, except perhaps 'tut, tut', but the sadness was etched on their faces as they passed by, the disappointment in their uplifted eyebrows as they heard a 'Padre' bid two diamonds or whatever. They would not have looked on bridge as frightfully wicked but as a wandering from the 'straight and narrow path', a dangerous lurching towards the 'wide gate, an easy way that leads to perdition'.

But these good, sincere people had more sadness and disappointment in store for them. Horse-racing of a sort took place on one of the decks about twice a week. Some of the missionaries of other denominations had reservations about the ethics of playing the

horses even though they were only toy horses. Toy horses powered
by electricity were for sale! One bought a horse for a few shillings
for each race. There was a tote system which gave odds on the different horses. As an owner who backed one's own horse, one was
deeply involved and shouted words of encouragement and affirmation to one's nag. This time the other denomination missionaries
expressed their disappointment, not only by their uplifted eyebrows but by sorrowful words of warning. At least, a lady missionary, a Scot, told me that what frightened her most was the wicked
looking faces of the Padres who owned horses and who frantically
urged their trusty steeds to get in there and win! Owning a horse, if
only for a few hours, was recreation and escape. All the same, the
good lady did see aggressiveness, competitiveness and perhaps a
little avarice – or at least the desire to win the race and the bet. She
saw all those things written on our faces. Whether they add up to
wickedness or not, I do not know. Perhaps wickedness, like beauty,
can sometimes be in the eye of the beholder.

With so many branches of the British Forces on board, it was inevitable that somebody should organise a tug-o-war competition. Air
Vice-Marshal Brown, who was the ranking Air Force officer on
board, became very friendly with us Padres. Jim Donohue and I
often walked with him on deck and he was a special friend of Jim's.
He was keen that the Padres should enter the tug-o-war competition. Our team consisted of seven priests and one Scotsman who
worked in a bank in Hong Kong. Presumably Air Vice-Marshal
Brown picked this man; in any case, it is always helpful to have a
banker around.

For the story of the competition, I shall now quote from one of the
Padres on board, Michael O'Neill, who wrote up the story in 1947
in the 'Far East', less than one year after the event. I quote, 'Each
contest in the event consisted of three pulls. To the huge amusement of the civilian passengers, to the astonishment of the troops
and to the still greater astonishment of ourselves, the missionary
tug-o-war team conquered all the others without conceding a single
pull. It was an interesting and unsuspected sidelight on missionary
versatility to see the Padres pulling the hardened veterans of
World War II down the deck. Jim Donohue, with his 16 stone 3lbs
was our anchor-man at the end of the rope and it would have
required a major military operation to shift him once he had

wrapped that rope around his broad back. Such an operation was not allowed under the rules of tug-o-war. I suppose the priests' team, for such it really was, averaged in weight about thirteen and a half stones. The ghosts of many a hard-fought hurling and football match in Dalgan (our seminary) must surely have hovered around the promenade deck on the day of the final. After this demonstration of muscular Christianity, we had some trouble in assuring the passengers of our peaceful intentions on coming to the Middle East.'

Air Vice-Marshal Brown, a man of between fifty and fifty-five years, with brown hair and moustache and of medium build and height, was thrilled. Less predictably, our fellow missionaries of other denominations were delighted at the outcome. Here was a brand of Christianity with which they could identify, a muscular brand if you like, and they could identify with it without raising an eyebrow or emitting a 'tut, tut'. Competing against us we had the Marines, Commandos, men of the Fleet Air Arm, Air Force, Navy and a number of military regiments. The Padres were very fit physically. They had cycled a lot round the parishes where they had served in England, Ireland and Wales during World War II.

But we must get on with our journey to China or we'll never reach there. When we sailed into the Red Sea, we found, as others have found, that it was like a hot brick wall; the temperature was 106°F and there was not a puff of air any place. Presumably anything more energetic would be too taxing, so for recreation a debate was arranged as we sailed through the Red Sea. There was nothing original about the motion of the debate which was 'Is suicide ever lawful?' I'm hazy about some aspects of that debate, but I do remember that most of those present were officers and men of the British Forces. The majority of them felt that suicide was lawful and indeed the only honourable course for a gentleman to follow when he has deserted his regiment or let down the side in some equally serious way.

When we reached the Indian Ocean there seemed to be so many whales around that I wonder now did we run into a school of whales on their mid-term break from further north. The leaping whales, rising from the ocean till they seemed to stand tiptoe on the waves and then spout fountains of spray before descending arc-like into the water again, were a delight to watch. I watched them so often that I now think of the Indian Ocean as a whale pond, where the whales kept anything but a low profile. I learned that the whale is related to the dolphin – kind of cousins – and I concluded that the entertainment business must run in the family. The dolphins are the comedians of the deep and their play-acting provided us with a lot of entertainment. They came quite close to the ship and, as we watched their antics, we had the feeling that they could see us and were playing to the gallery. But then, it is said, they rank next to humans in intelligence and like humans, they need that little bit of affirmation, applause and encouragement. The flying fish put on an act too. They glided considerable distances without touching the water. Apparently they can do up to 40 m.p.h. speeding through the air, a few feet above the water.

As we approached Singapore, I was eagerly looking out for – guess what? The Southern Cross. I have always been fascinated by the fact that the cross was in the sky since the stars were created. In my mind, I have always linked up the Southern Cross with the Emperor Constantine's experience. He is supposed to have seen the cross in the heavens before the battle of Milvian Bridge and to have seen the words near the Cross, 'In hoc signo vinces' (In this sign you shall conquer). Constantine became the first Christian Emperor. I have also linked the Southern Cross with something that appears in the Imitation of Christ. In that book we read that the Cross will appear in the heavens when Our Lord comes to judge us. However, I am told that lots of people do not believe the story about Constantine and that very few read the Imitation of Christ these days. But we still have the Southern Cross and my recollection is that an Englishman pointed it out to me in Singapore and that Singapore was the only place on our voyage that you could possibly see it. So there it was, hanging high and luminous in the October sky. It has been described as a small conspicuous constellation in the southern sky lying in the Milky Way. The four brightest stars of the constellation form a cross, the longer arm of which points roughly towards the South Pole.

In Singapore too, we saw thousands of Japanese prisoners, stripped to the waist, loading and unloading cargo in the harbour. We spent one night in Singapore and called at Raffles Hotel. Jim Donohue, Pat Brandon and I visited Kuala Lumpur. In Singapore,

an Anglo-Indian regiment which was bound for Hong Kong came
aboard. Air Vice-Marshal Brown and Jim Donohue and I were
walking the promenade deck one day and he told us about them
and told us too that he was anxious that we should have a tug-o-
war contest with them. He informed us that they were anxious to
meet the champions – the Padres Team – and so a contest was
arranged.

The night before the contest, while Jim Donohue, the captain of the
Padres Team, and I were taking the air on the promenade deck this
giant of a man in Anglo-Indian officer's uniform came up to us. He
tells us that he is captain of the Anglo-Indian tug-o-war team and
that he wants to clarify a few details about the contest. Business finished, we talked a little about this and that and before the Anglo-
Indian departed, Jim looked up at him and said, 'You are one of the
few men I have ever looked up to'. I thought this very funny
indeed, because the Anglo-Indian was 7' 4", the tallest man I have
ever seen, whereas Jim in comparison was a diminutive 6' 3". So I
erupted into an outburst of uncontrollable laughter in which Jim
joined. The Anglo-Indian was far from being amused. To our surprise, he was very annoyed. We thought it was a harmless kind of
joke, but he talked down to us in an aggressive manner and stated
that he could not see anything funny about the situation. As he
stomped off, he said slowly and deliberately, 'We will show you
Irishmen tomorrow.' The Anglo-Indian officer expected, I suppose,
a gravity of demeanour in the captain of a champion tug-o-war
team and he found this gravity lacking in Jim. For Jim, there was a
time for gravity in his life, but ordinarily, levity played a bigger
part in his dealings with people. The Anglo-Indians were more
Anglo than Indian; I think they were all white.

Here is the result of the contest, as it appeared in the ship's newspaper the next day. I quote, 'The Padres took the Anglo-Indian tug-o-
war team for a ride around the promenade deck'.

Somehow everybody seemed to be in better form and more sociable
as a result of that tug-o-war contest. Moustachioed officers of the
'stiff upper lip' persuasion, strict observance, became more talka-
tive and would say to us, as we met on the deck, 'Jolly good show
seeing off those Anglo-Indian chaps'. Our fellow missionaries of
other Christian persuasions were again delighted at the outcome

and they were so enthusiastic that you could almost hear the strains of 'Onward Christian Soldiers' in their enthusiasm. Steeped as they were in the Old Testament, some of them made a comparison between Jim Donohue and the Anglo-Indian on one hand and David and Goliath on the other. The comparison was apt enough as far as it went, but it fell short of reality by 2' 5" because Goliath was 9' 6", according to the Dictionary of the Bible. The Anglo-Indian captain was a mere 7' 4"!

There was another unexpected sequel to the Anglo-Indian contest. John Crowe, I believe, and Jim Donohue and I, were walking on the promenade deck when Air Vice-Marshal Brown joined us. He walked for a while with us and then invited us to come to his quarters where he could talk to us privately. In his office, he told us that the convincing way we had seen off the Anglo-Indians and indeed the other teams in the tug-o-war competition, gave him great pleasure. Our presence and our participation in organised games had helped the morale of all. Though not of our Church, he was very indebted to us, he said. Here he lowered his voice, although the door was shut, and began to whisper in almost a conspiratorial manner, 'As you know there is no hard liquor obtainable on this ship as wartime conditions still prevail. It is a dashed nuisance really. However, I have managed to get a case of Scotch for you boys,' and he beamed as he said this. 'There are eighteen Padres and there is just enough of Scotch whisky so that each of you can have a few drinks on me, in the days from here to Shanghai. It is a small token of my gratitude.' Again he beamed that smile so full of goodness on us. 'If word of this ever gets round then I will be deeply in the soup, so I ask you to be very discreet'.

His kindness left us speechless; for the first and last time on that voyage, we were at a loss for words, because we had worked in England and Wales and knew what wartime conditions meant. How were we to explain to this very kind gentleman that we were all Pioneers, total abstainers? We tried to explain to him what being a Pioneer meant, but I think we did not do it very well. He was gracious and understanding but, I think, mystified also. Here were eighteen young Irishmen and they were drinking nothing stronger than mineral water. That was something he found rather hard to swallow!

In Hong Kong, Air Vice-Marshal Brown invited the tug-o-war team to dinner in a British Officers Club. He requested the orchestra to play Irish music, but the only piece they had in their repertoire was 'When Irish Eyes are Smiling' and they kept repeating it. Some of the other British Officers present got tired of the repetition and protested. The Air Vice Marshal, however, outranked the other officers and kept to his piece, I am told. I was not on the tug-o-war team and so was not at the meal.

As the voyage progressed, all of us got to understand and appreciate our fellow travellers better. After the Anglo-Indian contest, it seemed to me that we Scots, English, Irish, as well as Welsh, suddenly discovered that we were all Europeans and that what we had in common was more considerable than what divided us. Perhaps it was that European Community man, St Columban, who was smiling down on us. Cardinal Ó Fiaich has described St Columban, our Patron, as 'Ireland's first European'. Robert Schumann, a French statesman, has said that St Columban is patron of those who seek to construct a united Europe. (St Columban, 540-615).

We had to go into Asia to discover we were Europeans. With our fellow missionaries of other denominations, there was a similar process at work during the voyage, so that by the time we came to journey's end, we were quite friendly. We began to appreciate their dedication, the long lives of service that many of them had given and their great Christian compassion. Being in the same boat for six weeks and being seasick forged a bond between us and produced a Christian fellowship of sorts. When we disembarked at Whangpoo, Shanghai, we were grateful that we had met our fellow travellers on the voyage and hoped we would meet them again.

Culture Shock

The coolies at the docks were on strike when we landed in Shanghai. Once again, Air Vice-Marshal Brown came to our aid and got the Air Force to unload our luggage. The coolies, however, were not a bit happy with this arrangement and when the Bursar from our Columban house in Shanghai came to meet us, he paid the coolies what they would have got if they had unloaded our luggage.

Our Bursar hired a truck into which we put our luggage. We sat on top of the truck dressed in our full clericals as it was getting wintery in Shanghai. The Columban house was in the French concession. The countries who had concessions were not bound by the laws of China but by the laws of their own countries while in Shanghai. The educated Chinese were very unhappy and felt very humiliated with this type of colonialism. They did not realise, I suppose none of us did at the time, that World War II had sounded the death knell of colonialism.

On route to the Columban House in Rue Maresca, from our vantage point on the top of the truck we noted the cosmopolitan and commercial character of Shanghai. On either side of the river bank were houses, go-downs or warehouses and factories whose tall chimneys were belching forth smoke. On the wide dirty river there was a large assortment of shipping which ranged from the sampan and small native cargo-carrying junks to the ocean-going steamers. The intimidating skyscrapers which lined the Bund seemed strangely out of place in an oriental city. The Sikh security guards and policemen were much in evidence.

Our house in Rue Maresca, Shanghai, was the Columban headquarters for Asia. At that time, our missions in Asia were in Burma, China, Korea and Japan. The house was called The Procure because goods were bought in Shanghai and shipped up to our missions in the interior of China and even sometimes to Korea. Greeting us when we arrived were two American Columbans on their way to the States for vacation from Hanyang, and two Australian Columbans on their way to Hanyang after a vacation in Australia. It was great meeting our fellow missionaries from America and Australia and in the next few weeks there was a lot of fun, banter and practical jokes. We identified with them as Columban Brothers almost instantly and soon felt as if we had known them all our lives. The two Americans were bright young men, outgoing and witty, John Healy and John Breakey.

The two Australian priests were somewhat older than us and the Americans. Gerry O'Collins had a flourishing beard and, like his hair, it was an iron grey. Both Gerry and Pat Hennessy had been in prison during the Japanese occupation and they had suffered quite a bit. Gerry had bad health and looked emaciated. He did not have to return to China, he told us, but wanted to do so, to encourage us younger missionaries. That was typical of the man. Pat Hennessy was a quiet man, but very strong and healthy.

In Dalgan, we always looked forward to Old China hands coming on vacation who would tell us outlandish stories about China. We didn't want to hear stories that sounded commonplace, we wouldn't be interested in them. Gerry O'Collins' stories, when he came, were first class. In Shanghai, he told us about his ill health. In 1933, he had been hospitalised in Hankow and he was so ill that he was advised to take his coffin up the country with him. A weak heart was his problem. The bad heart dogged him all his days until finally it failed him at the age of 83 after he had done a great life's work.

In those days, the challenge of China was strongly felt in missionary circles. Missionaries were converging on Shanghai from many European countries and from Australia and America en route to their mission stations in the interior of China. It is hard to realise now that what the Himalayas was to mountaineers, China was to the missionary societies in 1946. The Director of our mission in Asia, an Australian, Fr Bill McGoldrick, was away the night that we arrived. He came back the second day and after supper he kindly offered to play the piano. He played 'Waltzing Matilda' and called for a vocalist. But there was no vocalist, or at least one who know the words of 'Waltzing Matilda'.

The Columban Sisters, who are very dedicated missionaries and are deeply imbued with the spirit of St Columban, had a convent and a very interesting apostolate in Shanghai at this time. They looked after the spiritual needs of the emigré Russian Catholics of the Oriental Rite who had fled to Shanghai during the Stalin oppression. Each Sunday, the Russian Catholics came to the Columban Sisters' church for their Russian Rite liturgy. The priests who were looking after them, and who were experts on the Russian liturgy, were English Jesuits, Fr Wilcock and Fr O'Brannigan. Most of the Sundays we were in Shanghai, we would go down to the Columban Sisters' Church for the Russian liturgy after we had said Mass in our own house. It took about two and a half hours, but it was very beautiful.

During our stay in Shanghai, seven of us were appointed to Hanyang diocese where Bishop Galvin, our Co-Founder, was bishop, and six of us were appointed to Nancheng where Bishop Cleary was bishop. Of the remaining five, four were assigned to Korea and one to Japan. The five would do their language studies in our Shanghai house. Then quite unexpectedly, as we were starting tiffin on the 23rd November, the feast of St Columban – of all days – the voice of the Bursar was to be heard making an announcement. He told us that the Yangtse boat was waiting and that it would leave at once.

We rushed out from tiffin in mid-fruit-cocktail and hastened to the Whangpoo. When we got on board, we noticed that there were some Dominican Sisters, Americans, amongst the passengers. There were also some American soldiers and a few civilians. There were no signs, that we could see, that the boat was leaving soon. Seven hours later the boat was still there and we were getting rather hungry. In the nick of time, a meal was provided for us. After the meal, we watched the sunset and then proceeded to play poker. The Dominican Sisters thought we should have Mass quite early the next morning so as to be ready for an early start. We did this, but the boat showed no sign of starting – early or late.

Shanghai is not China; it is a modern cosmopolitan city and has been called the Paris of the East, but when we entered that L.S.T. boat (Landing Ship Tanks) anchored on the Yangtse, we entered China. To our consternation, we noted that the boat was not merely unpunctual, it was a non-starter for about a week. We had been brought up in a European culture where the importance of punctuality was paramount. We had been trained to keep our engagements on the dot or a little before it and to expect the same from our people. We were told that you had to be punctual if you wanted to get on. Here in the boat on the Yangtse, we were being absorbed into a 3,000 year old culture where the people were more interested in the art of living than in the art of getting on.

It is a painful experience being absorbed into a new culture. Nowadays they call it 'culture shock'. That boat in which we found ourselves on the Yangtse was a kind of a time machine in which we were levered back into the 19th Century where the tempo was so much slower. Frantic, rushing and hectic hurrying had no place in the new century and the new culture in which we found ourselves.

Before we left Shanghai, the Communist threat seemed so imminent that other missionary societies were sending their young men back to Shanghai from the interior. The jokes going round the missionary procures in Shanghai were that the young Columbans were going up the river, while the young men of other missionary societies were coming down. The rumours did not worry us and indeed we would not have thought of them at all, only that our boat was such a slow starter.

Eventually, just about a week after we rushed out from our Columban Day tiffin with such undignified haste to catch a boat which was about to leave, our voyage up the Yangtse began. The Yangtse is the third longest river in the world, beaten only by the Amazon and the Congo. It is nearly 3,500 miles long and sometimes has been called the 'wicked river', because so many have died when the river flooded over the years and over the centuries. The sounds one hears on the Yangtse come back to my mind and the one that I particularly remember is the plaintive chant of the boat men in small boats making their way upstream from Shanghai. 'Ai... Yo. Ai...Yo,' is how the chant seemed to sound.

Sailing the Yangtse was pleasant enough and the river was dotted with all kinds of shipping ranging from sampans to river steamers like our own. We stopped briefly at Anking, and the capital of China as it then was, Nanking. By day we chatted with the Sisters or with some of the American soldiers and the time passed quickly. On the horizon, one could sometimes see thatched huts and women and children watching over landing nets and lowering the nets into the water in an effort to catch fish.

We watched the splendid sunsets also. It took us some time to get used to the fact that in the Orient there is no twilight and after the sunsets, darkness comes down with the swiftness of a blow – of a karate chop, it seemed to me. That magic moment when the sun goes down over the Yangtse, leaving in the waters a trail of silver light, has been caught by countless Chinese painters and artists. In every sunset, there is a hint of our mortality but in the Oriental sunsets the hint is more pointed and pronounced because the sun sets so swiftly.

About five days after we set out, we reached the port of Kukiang where we who were going to Nancheng were scheduled to disembark. Formerly, Kukuang had been an important port on account of the tea trade, but now was in a state of decline.

After we docked, two bearded European missionaries came on board the river steamer. They had long, dark Chinese gowns and Chinese caps. They introduced themselves to us as Fr Larry Morrell, a Frenchman, who was in charge of the Vincentian compound in Kukiang and Fr Pat O'Connell, a Columban Missionary. The latter I think found himself stranded in Kukiang when the Japanese war broke out and stayed there for the duration. During that time, he had to speak either Chinese or French. As soon as he saw us he was determined to show Larry Morrell that he had a language of his own and addressed us loudly in Irish. He was a most interesting talker and told us about his experience of teaching in a Chinese middle school in Kukiang and of his years as a missionary in Hanyang, where he had been beaten, stabbed and gagged by bandits or communists. He wanted to hear any news there was from Ireland. And after we gave it to him, he returned to telling us of his own experiences. He must have been near sixty when we met him. As a young priest, he had been a professor of Irish in St Finian's College in Mullingar. He talked of the revival of the Irish language and of the Celtic renaissance and as he was really getting lost in his subject, we were brought down to earth without any warning when the boat seemed to be pulling out from Kukiang. We rushed to the gangway and disembarked and had our luggage sent after us.

Larry Morrell and Pat then took us to the Vincentian compound and there we had a meal and further conversation. Larry Morrell told us he had been thirty years in China without returning to France and that he had served as a soldier in the French Army in World War I. After we had a wash and a siesta, we met again. Pat reminisced about his days as a Maynooth student. The Columbans originated in the Seminary of Maynooth. Our two co-founders were Maynooth men and one of them, John Blowick, was a brilliant professor. Pretty well all the early Columbans were Maynooth men too, and so in the beginning it was natural that our Missionary Society should be called the Maynooth Mission to China.

We stayed up quite late that night, later than we should actually, because Larry Morrell had told us that we could say Mass the next morning between 4.30 and 5.00. We thought that a bit early because for some of us, in our pre-China days, the crack of noon had been a much more familiar landmark than the crack of dawn.

After breakfast, we loaded our luggage on the two small trucks which Larry Morrell had hired for us, to take to Nanchang, the capital of Jiangsi province. The journey was miserable and we got drenched by the heavy rains. At night we had to sleep in the trucks to guard our possessions and we reached Nanchang at the end of the second day. There we found an American Columban, Bob Degnan, waiting for us and welcoming us and he took us to the Vincentian procure. The Archbishop of Nanchang, who was a Chinese Vincentian, and the rest of the Vincentian community, were very hospitable. Most of the conversation took place in colloquial Latin as our French was not that good. Towards the end of the meal, a Dutch Vincentian asked me the inevitable question, 'Is half-past four too late for you to say Mass tomorrow morning?' I fear I dodged the question and referred him to another member of our group who sat at the end of the table. The priest to whom I referred him needed two alarm clocks to waken him in the morning and indeed sometimes two alarm clocks and a missionary. He gave the Dutchman every possible assurance that half past four was not too late.

Early the next morning, we started out on the last leg of our journey. Bob Degnan had hired a few trucks for our luggage and we reached Nancheng about four o'clock that afternoon. The Catholic compound which the Columbans had inherited from the French

Vincentians seemed to be rather large. It contained the cathedral, a seminary, a primary school, a hospital, a dispensary, a convent, an orphanage and an old peoples' home. Bishop Cleary, who was first bishop of Nancheng, the Columban Sisters and priests, both foreign and Chinese, gave us a very warm welcome. After a wash and change of clothes, we sat down to a meal not, as we had expected, of all kinds of exotic Chinese dishes, but to a meal of bacon, eggs, bread and coffee, provided by the Columban Sisters. The food, the living quarters, everything was much better than we had dared to expect. One of our group writing to me recently said that that evening in Nancheng was the happiest of his adult life.

Some of the priests attached to the Nancheng seminary we had known in the seminary in Ireland and then it was a matter of renewing old friendships. The Bishop, however, we had not known previously except by reputation and his reputation was a formidable one. He was tall, slim, scholarly, elegant in manner and appearance and a Christian gentleman. He had been a Professor of Theology in Maynooth College when our Missionary Society was formed. In less than two years, he had joined us and was soon made Rector of the new seminary. His task was to give suitable formation to young men in the seminary who had volunteered for missionary work in China. For various reasons, priests working in China would depend on each other to a far greater extent than priests working in the home country. So the first objective he aimed at was to produce a strong Columban brotherhood, an esprit de corps, which would help the young men in the Seminary and later help them in China when they were ordained.

Under Bishop Cleary, and indeed before he came to Dalgan, examinations were not superintended because the seminarians were left to their honour. They studied not because they were being watched by a Dean or Professors, but because they were very conscious of the presence of God. Being left on their honour during examinations and indeed during their seminary days, was called the Honour System. We had heard that the system worked rather well in the seminary when Bishop Cleary was Rector. He had that rare ability of getting the best out of each boy and I suppose his kindness and understanding helped a lot. We were told that the same Honour System worked very well in the diocese in China where he was in charge.

The first night, as we sat round and had a bit of crack, Bishop Cleary just listened, laughed at the jokes and enjoyed his pipe. As we watched him that night, we could not help thinking that he measured up to St Peter's expectations when the latter was exhorting the elders on how they should behave to those under them (1 Pet 3:5). Peter's words are, 'Not as domineering over those in your charge but being examples to the flock'.

Believe it or not, it was a cocoa session we had that night – nothing stronger – and the crack seemed to get better after the second cup of cocoa. The Bishop told the odd story, but for the most part asked questions about home. As he said, he was a theologian by trade but Scripture was his first and last love. He was deeply interested in English literature and asked about the latest books. When we disbanded about 11.00 p.m., we newcomers felt very happy about the spirit of the community we had joined.

We had travelled hopefully for nearly 12,000 miles in almost nine weeks. But travelling hopefully is not better than to have arrived when you have the good fortune to have arrived at the Catholic Mission in Nancheng.

CHAPTER 3

Old Curiosity Shop

Next morning some of the priests took us out to see the city of Nan-cheng and what a devastated city it was. The city was burnt by the Japanese army during the Sino-Japanese War in 1942. Even the Catholic mission hospital did not escape, though all the other buildings in the Catholic compound escaped the devastation. In that compound we noticed a lot of activity. The Columban Sisters ran an orphanage very efficiently and also an old people's home. Refugees from the war days were still living in the compound and a makeshift hospital and dispensary were doing very effective work. Then there was the seminary with upwards of 40 Chinese boys and it seemed a very happy place, and there was a primary school with a few hundred Catholic Chinese children on the roll. In the Cathedral parish they had a number of catechists; about a hundred Chinese were to be baptised into the Catholic church the following Easter. One of the Columban Sisters was a nurse, one was engaged in pastoral activities, one ran the orphanage and another made bread for the outlying missions and sent it to them as opportunity served.

At tiffin, there was a lot of lively repartee as we related to the bishop and to the priests what we thought of China. One Job's comforter told us not to worry about the language because, he said, the first twenty years learning Chinese is always the toughest anyhow. For the next few days the bishop and the priests told us about their experiences. Practically all of them had great admiration for the Chinese people and specifically for the ones they knew best, the Catholics. After only a few days in the country, we could see that the Chinese we had met were extremely polite and courteous. The men who had been in China up to twenty years assured us that the Chinese were people of heroic patience, that contentment came to them easily and that their equanimity in all circumstances was re-markable. Of course, we were reminded that they had three or four thousand years of civilisation behind them and that this contributed to their calm, passive strength and mellow humour. The Bishop informed us that between Chinese businessmen there was no need for written agreements. A businessman's word was his bond.

Bishop Cleary felt that he should not only preach but also put into practice the Papal Encyclicals on Social Justice. For that reason, he paid those who worked in his compound what he thought was a just living wage. It turned out be a much higher wage than that paid to people in similar jobs in Nancheng city. Indeed, some of his priests criticised him on this score. The Bishop believed that foreigners, on the whole, tended to give less than living wages to houseboys and compradores and then to blame them when they took what was called a 'commission'.

About a week after our arrival in Nancheng, each of us newcomers was appointed to country parishes. The men who had served in the Sino-Japanese War needed a holiday and so we were unable to go to school and study the language together. We had to try to study Chinese individually, helped by a local teacher in the parishes to which we were assigned. It was far from ideal as a system but it was the best we could do in the circumstances. I was appointed to a town about half the size of Nancheng and forty miles south – Lichuan. The parish priest was Father Ned Byrne from County Down and the other curate was Father Jack De Rosier, a Columban from Windsor, Ontario. The living conditions were about the same as they were in Nancheng. The teacher assigned to help me learn the language was Benedict and he was good but I fear I was not a good pupil.

Bishop Cleary advised us to keep our eyes open during our first six months in China and to observe and write down anything that seemed strange or bizarre to us in the Chinese way of doing things and in Chinese customs. If we did not write them down, we would forget them later. If we did not observe such strange things in the first six months, we would take them for granted afterwards. I fear I made more progress at observing the Chinese than at learning their language.

Here are some of the things I noticed in January and February 1947:

A Chinese book is read from top to bottom, from right to left and from back to front.

When addressing envelopes they put the country first, then the county, then the town and afterwards the person's name.

They drink wine hot, never warm or cold.

They swing the spade over their heads when digging; the spade is like a pick-axe with a broad head.

If a teacher in this part of the world wants to summon a child, the teacher raises the hand palm upwards and waggles the index finger. In China, they raise the hand palm downwards and waggle the four fingers in unison.

In China the guest of honour is put on the left, not on the right.

The host does not shake hands with his guest: he shakes his own hands together as a sign of welcome.

Men wear their hats in company.

Brides wear scarlet, not white.

We say 'whoa' when we want a horse to stop; they say 'whoa' when they want a horse to start.

They get into the saddle from the right, not from the left.

In their compasses the black arrow points to the south, not to the north and points read east, west, south, north.

At their banquets they begin with the dessert and finish with the soup.

Their mentality and their approach to so many of the everyday activities of life is diametrically opposed to ours. To my Chinese friends, comparisons of this kind were highly amusing and not at all odious. Their keen perception of the comic and incongruous lightened for these poor people the heavy burden of precarious living. I have heard them laugh heartily when I have told them that in my little country people bring thread to the needle. In China, they bring the needle to the thread. But when the laughter subsided, they explained that for people who did things in ways different from theirs, they had understanding and sympathy.

White is the colour of mourning, funerals are noisy affairs and there are coffins and coffins. Let me explain. Shortly after I reached the curacy to which Bishop Cleary appointed me, I noticed something which to me seemed extraordinary. My first morning there I noticed a large, empty, elegant-looking Chinese coffin leaning against the compound wall, near the back door of the Church. That afternoon I saw an elderly but vigorous-looking Chinese gentleman, dressed in a long blue gown and black and velvet skull cap, standing in the compound and gazing pensively at the coffin. His sparsely whiskered chin spoke of a Vandyke that had failed or at least had given only 30% or 40% yield. Having looked thoughtfully for a moment at the coffin, he tapped the lid with his fingers and ran his hands lingeringly along the sides. Each afternoon the ritual was repeated.

I was so busy asking about other novelties that it was some time before I enquired about the coffin. When I did make enquiries the parish priest, Ned Byrne, informed me that the old man had deliberately, and with much forethought, bought the coffin many years earlier. It gives one 'face' to have one's coffin ages before one's funeral. The longer the coffin is left to season, the better wear it will give, hopefully. The old man tapped the coffin to see how it was seasoning. The more elegant and massive the coffin, the bigger the face the owner will have during life and after death.

In China people can get coffin-proud. If one has an expensive coffin seasoning at the back of one's house, one need never run short of subject matter for boasting. A missionary who had spent twenty years in China told me he heard a Chinese merchant boasting that he had bought the most expensive coffin in his native town or for miles around it. He claimed that it would take up to twenty men to carry this coffin at his funeral and that it was made from the rarest wood in the Province of Hubei. But even the coffin-proud have their own troubles in this sad world. The fact that one has an expensive coffin seasoning nicely behind one's house does not mean that it's all plain sailing to the cemetery. I heard that a wandering beggar on his last legs may get into such a coffin and appropriate it. Such an occupant cannot be ousted; the owner would lose big face if he attempted an eviction. The erstwhile proud owner has to stand idly by while somebody else goes off with his coffin, so to speak.

Notice how I could not write a paragraph on coffins without mentioning 'face' three or four times. In my sadly depleted collection of 'Chinoiserie' 'face' is by far the most fascinating item. Till one knows something about 'face' one can understand little about China. Not that anybody understands fully what 'face' is. According to Lin Yu Tang, the Chinese author, it is an abstract and intangible thing and really 'face' is indefinable. It is a bit like prestige, a bit like dignity but some of its manifestations have little in common with either idea. Status can be acquired and sustained and social relations regulated by 'face'. 'Face' enters into every department of life and brings a new dimension to the Chinese scene. Saving 'face', getting 'face' is of first importance, losing 'face' can be a calamity.

Here, however, the Chinese themselves tell stories which are calculated to throw some light on the nature and nuances of 'face'. This is one which appears in a number of books on China. In the early days of the Manchu Dynasty, in the town of Woonang, a cat-burglar, whom we shall call Wong of Celestial Virtue, entered the house of a poor man by night. He had heard that there was nobody home so he abandoned the 'cat-like tread' which he usually employed when entering a house. Fancy his surprise on lighting up his torch to find the poor man in bed. Worse still, he noticed the poor man shutting his eyes and pretending to be asleep. This gave Celestial Virtue pause and he said to himself, 'He has seen that I was going to steal and he doesn't want me to lose face so he pretends to be asleep.' What beautiful manners! And Celestial Virtue, reverting to the cat-like tread of his profession, tip-toed out of the house when the poor man thought to himself, 'the thief sees that I'm very poor and wants to spare me. By so doing he will make me lose face.' And the poor man cried out, 'Esteemed thief, I'm a poor man but please do not go away without stealing something – if it's only chopsticks – otherwise I shall have no 'face' in town tomorrow.'

The story has a couple of noteworthy aspects. The thief puts 'face' before business and the man with few worldly goods would rather lose some of them than lose 'face'. I suppose 'face' derives directly from Confucius and from the pre-Confucian rites, 'Keep your own status and resign yourself to heaven's will', says the Sage. Celestial Virtue and the poor man in the story, each of them in his own way, is trying to keep his proper status.

'Face', too, can turn up in the most unexpected places and in the most unlikely situations. Which reminds me of the time I had to ride a choleric, devious, intransigent and really vicious mule twenty miles so that the owner would not lose face. To be quite fair, the owner found the mule docile and always well-disposed. I should also say that I very much appreciated the kind thought which prompted him to offer me the mule. He wanted to spare me the hardship of walking twenty miles through the sodden bridle-path in and out of Nancheng. Other things being equal, to have been offered a mule for such a journey on a cold and wet February day looked an attractive proposition. I have since learned that other things are seldom equal when there's a Mongolian mule in the equation. But I am running ahead of my story. It happened in the Chinese New Year of 1949. An old Chinese priest gave an excellent Mission in my little parish. He was having breakfast with some relatives in the village the morning the Mission ended when somebody told him I might be going to Nancheng that day. Immediately he said that I would have to take his mule and he showed his relatives the tins of American tobacco which I had given him and for which he was very grateful. Soon one of his relatives came to me with the message about the mule. I thanked the Chinese priest for his kind offer but asked to be excused. Back came the messenger at once saying that I should take the mule, that it was a matter of 'face' as the mule had been offered to me publicly. So I agreed. I wouldn't dream of letting the old Chinese priest, who had given such an excellent Mission, lose face. If 'face' were to be lost it was the priest in charge who should lose it, not the visitor. Unfortunately I didn't have a curate.

Well, the mule was brought round and from the word go things went wrong. When I attempted to get into the saddle from the left side, the houseboy whispered that you mount from the right side in China. By now the inevitable Chinese crowd had gathered. As I went round to mount from the right side, the mule threw a smart kick at me, which was only half-inches wide. I had my foot in the stirrup when he turned his head swiftly and took a king-sized bite at my right arm. Fortunately, I was wearing a leather jacket. I have very vivid memories of his long rows of ivory coloured teeth, like the keyboard of a small accordion. Eventually I did get in to the saddle and I don't blame the mule for not starting because I probably gave him the wrong signal. I certainly didn't say 'whoa' to him. The crowd, however, exhorted him in language he understood, the birch was produced, a little persuasion applied and soon we were on our way. Perhaps I'm allergic to mules, or perhaps it's vice versa. I am sorry to have to put on record that the kick and bite motif recurred in the mule's behavioural patterns whenever opportunity served. All through the journey he made frantic efforts to unseat me and it was more by good luck than good management on my part that he failed.

Once 'face' has been lost, the next step is to try to restore it. Firecrackers are the patent 'face' restorers. The Chinese invented gunpowder and let it be said to their credit that they used it largely as a face-giver or restorer ... up to recent times. When the young missionary comes to China, he is always amused at some of the manifestations of 'face'. A few years later that same missionary can become almost as 'face-minded' as the Chinese themselves. Shortly before we arrived in China, a certain Columban missionary lost 'face' with the local authorities in his parish. If you were passing by that missionary's compound gate early the morning after he lost 'face', your ears would be smitten with the rat-tat-tat-tat of firecrackers being let off. You would see the missionary in question solemnly standing to attention while the rite of face-restoring was being performed by his equally serious house-boy and the inevitable Chinese crowd gathering and passively following the proceedings. The 'face' thus restored could be pronounced equal to the 'face' lost. The happy ending to which all 'face' losers aspire had been reached.

I fear that during my first few months in Lichuan, I spent more time observing the people and the way they did things than studying the language. This was the advice that Bishop Cleary gave to us. During these few months, I came to the conclusion that China, as far as I was capable of giving an opinion on it, was the quaintest of 'Old Curiosity Shops'.

CHAPTER 4

Diner in Distress

In treating of ways and means of acquiring a proper spirit of humility and patience, ascetical writers seem to have overlooked the possibilities lurking in a pair of chopsticks.

I was only a few days in Lichuan when Ned Byrne, the pastor, Jackie Des Rosiers and I were invited to a 'chi chu' or Chinese banquet by the Mayor. Such invitations are generally welcomed and accepted by the priest as an opportunity of making contact with educated pagans and influential officials. Since the use of chopsticks is pretty well *de rigeur* at these functions, the record of one's early encounter with chopsticks becomes largely the story of the first few banquets one attends.

I was not eager to attend this Lichuan dinner and like the men in the Gospel who had been invited to the wedding feast, I began to make excuses. I pointed out that I had been only a few weeks in China; that I was unable to ply a decent chopstick; that my conversational knowledge of Chinese, consisting as it did of a thorough grasp of two sentences, could scarcely be regarded as an asset at any social gathering. But in the end, prompted by my curiosity I fear, I yielded to the entreaties of my would-be host and went to the feast.

As we entered the low-ceilinged, dimly-lighted room, all the guests stood up, bowed graciously and welcomed us. Ned Byrne was put in the place of honour. In the interchange of greetings I squandered half my stock of conversational Chinese, reserving the other half for a lull in the talk or some such emergency. Stools were placed for us around a circular table, four or five steaming bowls were carried in and set in the centre of the board, and the meal began.

In front of each guest lay a plate and a pair of brown innocent-looking chopsticks. The signal to commence was given by our host who raised his chopsticks aloft and held them over one of the bowls. In an atmosphere of ceremonious silence we all followed suit, holding our chopsticks poised at the same altitude. Then on the invitation to eat, 'Chin Chin', each made a simultaneous downward thrust at the bowl.

Everyone, except myself, succeeded in securing a morsel and conveying it to his plate. My chopsticks crossed and re-crossed each other, got in each other's way, went out of control and spreadeagled themselves over the table – did everything, in fact, except what they were supposed to do. After a few vain attempts, I decided to make a strategic withdrawal from the bowl, hoping that my retreat should escape notice under cover of small-talk all around. But no. I was detected by one of the guests who was on his way back for a second helping and who took it upon himself to give me a demonstration of the proper method of handling chopsticks. Under this tuition, I made some progress, so slight however that my further efforts, which by now had attracted the attention of the whole table, provoked outbursts of indulgent laughter in which I wholeheartedly joined. At this point my host, realising that I should never make a meal of it left to the mercy of my unfamiliar weapons, summoned an attendant to present me with a spoon. Never had I experienced such an uplift of heart at the sight of a mere spoon, even though its appearance meant that I had failed dismally in my first public attempt to dine *à la Chinoise*.

Meanwhile, fresh dishes were following one another in quick succession. Soon we had sampled nine or ten of which, being no expert in these matters, I can only say that they contained vegetables, fish and several kinds of meat. A medley of jingling rhymes from Belloc kept teasing and distracting me:

> 'What different tastes in food
> Divide the human brotherhood'.

and

> 'Birds in their little nests agree
> With Chinamen, but not with me'.

Not that I noticed any little birds, with or without their little nests; the nearest approach had been a boiled chicken which contrary to Irish usage, had appeared on the board 'armed with beak and claws'. Neither had I been able to distinguish the various kinds of meat, and when on one occasion I called across the table to Ned Byrne, 'What is that dish?' his non-committal reply, 'Ham to you, Father', so far from enlightening me only aroused my worst suspicions. But whatever their nature, I found all the dishes tasty and agreeable, and the experience made me wonder if the Chinese taste in food is as extraordinary as we of another tradition have always imagined it to be. At the very least we should give the Chinese credit for being neither narrow nor hide-bound in culinary matters. They look on the animal kingdom, snake, frog, dog etc., as their larder, in which nothing is either good or bad, but cooking makes it so. And their cooking, excellent as it is in itself, is further enhanced by that satellite art of which they are past masters – the art of flavouring. Their cooking-spit is the Great Leveller of the animal kingdom; their sauces convert indifferent fare into a morsel fit for a gourmet.

The resolve to make good with chopsticks asserted itself immediately on my arrival home after the banquet and I set out to improve my style. Following an old and well-tried system recommended by Ned Byrne, I laid ten matches in circular formation on the table and advancing in anti-clockwise direction, proceeded to lift them with the chopsticks. My first attempts were a repetition of my performance at the dinner, but gradually I began to improve and with increased confidence my progress was rapid. Soon the day came when I was able to lift, and convey upwards, seven out of ten matches at the first attempt.

At the next banquet my host complimented me on my improvement with the chopsticks. He encouraged me too by saying that, in due time, I would master the intricacies of the Chinese language as well!

Taking up the challenge, I decided to get up at 4.30 in the morning. like the French missionaries, and take the language-learning seriously. The evening before I started this new regime, I developed a Walter Mitty type of fantasy: I could see myself mastering a few characters and memorising quite a few phrases by tiffin. Not only that, but I could also see myself correcting some of the other missionaries when they got the tones wrong, etc..

But even in my fantasy, I could not forget that the Chinese language has about 40,000 characters and that some of the characters are made up of as many as twenty strokes. Nor could I forget that Blessed Gabriel Perboyre C.M., a French missionary, who worked in our area in China in the last century, wrote that the Chinese language was 'inventio diaboli', an invention of the devil. But that did not worry me while the fantasy lasted. I was up at the crack of dawn next morning and after meditation, Mass and breakfast, looked forward with glee to five hours of uninterrupted and rewarding study.

The fantasy world, however, ended and I landed with a thud in the harsh world of reality round the crack of noon. Before tiffin I had an opportunity of assessing how rewarding and uninterrupted my five hours study was in actual fact. To my horror, I discovered that it was not rewarding because I had not mastered one Chinese character or one Chinese phrase. St Paul could say, 'I can will what is right, but I cannot do it,' and he didn't have to learn Chinese. For the future, I would be more modest in my plans and I would speak to the children and listen to them and imitate pronunciations and tones where possible.

**

Around this time, I got a pain in the chest and the doctor in Nancheng, a Chinese doctor said that I had a bad heart and that I should not walk more than three li, which is the equivalent of a mile. It was decided that I should go to Shanghai to see a foreign doctor.

There was a new bunch of missionaries in our house in Shanghai when I got there and they were all contemporaries of my own and the crack was very good. I went to see the doctor, a religious man of the Orthodox Russian faith, and he trained his stethoscope on me. Having listened carefully for a minute or two he said, 'You are smoking too many cigarettes'. When I answered that I did not smoke cigarettes at all, only the pipe, he was rather perplexed. Then he listened a little harder and after another few minutes he said, half apologetically, 'I hope you don't mind me saying this but you had better take it easy on the bottle'. Now it was my turn to be perplexed so I said, 'Doctor, I don't drink, I'm a Pioneer'. Then he got annoyed and listened through the stethoscope a little longer. Then he said, just that little bit testily, I thought, 'You will drink from now on'. Well, I suppose, there have been other 'U-turns' like this in the history of diagnosis but I had not heard of any of them. So I asked him, 'Doctor, what have you in mind?' He replied, 'You are living under a state of great tension up in the interior of China. The Communists are advancing, bandits are on the prowl. What I want you to do is to stay in Shanghai for six weeks and before tiffin and before your evening meal, take two large tablespoonfuls of Whiskey'. No one could say that the doctor had prescribed to excess. Two close friends, the late John Crowe and Art Friel, who were both afterwards missionaries in Japan, had accompanied me and were waiting anxiously outside the surgery when I came out. When I related to them what the doctor had prescribed, they greeted my remarks with hoots of laughter. However, I invited them to lunch to a Chinese restaurant and when they saw me order the first draught of the prescription, they no longer doubted but were believing. When we returned to the Columban house that afternoon, my two friends told the story to everybody. All who heard it laughed loudly but most were Doubting Thomases. Whiskey on prescription! Well, with the good company and the comparatively relaxed atmosphere in Shanghai, I made steady progress and after a month was in good shape.

Our General Chapter, which had just finished, decided that we must buy a house in Beijing. They further decided that every Columban missionary assigned to China should go to Peking and learn the language there for two or three years as the Franciscans, who ran the school, would advise. It was felt that once a priest had gone through the language school and learned Mandarin that he could easily master the dialect of the mission to which he was assigned in China. All that made a lot of sense. However, when we heard the disturbing news that the Communists were beating at the gates of Beijing we began to wonder if we should not wait a bit. Priests who had served in China for a number of years told us that there were always rumours of wars in China and if one waited till there were rumours of peace, one never did anything. While all this was undoubtedly true, the Reds at this time seemed to be moving with discipline and determination and other old China hands shook their heads sadly.

About my fifth week in Shanghai, the Bursar from Nancheng came to Shanghai for supplies. He bought a consignment of Mass wine and oatmeal and other things that could not be bought in Nancheng. He hired a box car on the train which would take him most of the way back and he invited me to make the return journey with him. We expected to be back in Nancheng in about four days.

While I was in Shanghai, I got news that I had been appointed to teach in the Major Seminary in Nancheng. Most of the lectures in the Major Seminary were given in Latin. I was very amused at the appointment, as indeed were my contemporaries. My big qualification for the job was that I could mimic the professors who lectured us in Latin in the seminary, fairly adequately and at some length. One of the professors had a great flow of Latin and my classmates and I were always impersonating him and suddenly we found that some of us had become fairly fluent in Latin too.

Jim Yang, a Chinese priest trained and ordained by Bishop Cleary, was also on the staff. A few years earlier, when he was about thirty. he had got a degree in Chinese Civil Law at Amoy University.

The Rector of the seminary was an American, Pat Gately, and life there was quite interesting. As well as speaking Chinese, most of the Chinese priests could speak Latin and English (and a few spoke French as well) so there was something to be said for keeping Latin in the Seminary. Any missionary you met in China, no matter what his nationality was, even if you did not understand his Chinese, you could always converse with him in Latin.

CHAPTER 5

Rumours of War

We had been aware of the danger of the communist threat for some months. However, I feel that the danger really registered with me when I had a letter from my friend Fr Jim Donohue (who had been the anchor man of our tug-o-war team on board the Empress of Australia). He had been transferred to the Diocese of Hanyang in Hubei some months earlier. In his letter, which I received in early January 1948, he described the arrival of the Reds in the northern part of the Diocese and a close escape he and Bishop Galvin had. They fled before the oncoming communist army and reached Hanyang City just in the nick of time. I read out the letter at tiffin the day I received it. Present were Bishop Cleary, Jim Yang, Ted Mac Elroy and others. 'That is news,' said the Bishop, his eyes wide with amazement. Then for a moment there was silence. John Chang, a Chinese priest was first to speak. 'So the Reds are in Hubei Province,' he said, 'only the River Yangtse between us and the communists now.' 'The river is a big obstacle and let's hope an insuperable one,' said the Bishop, as he pulled at his pipe and warmed his hands on a tea-cosy.

But even though the communists and ourselves were separated only by the Yangtse River, many of the older missionaries and indeed many of the Chinese with whom we talked, were convinced that the Americans would never allow the communists to cross the Yangtse. They couldn't allow them to do so, it was said, in their own interests. To allow them to cross the Yangtse would be to hand them south China on a platter.

Midst the rumours and alarms which continued through Spring and Summer, the older men reminded us that in 1928 a communist state was set up with its headquarters in Jiangsi. It extended into western Fujian, as well. At one time or another it had been extended to include parts of Guangdong and Hubei. We learned, too, how Fr

Tim Leonard, the first Columban martyr, was killed by the communists in July 1929. He was pastor of Nanfeng, about 30 miles south of Nancheng. The communist guerillas had made a raid on the town and his information seemed to have been that they had left at dawn on this particular day in July. He decided to ring the bell to inform the people that morning Mass would take place as usual. The bell attracted the attention of some of the communist stragglers and they decided to fire shots through a window into the church. Mick Moran, who was a curate in the Nanfeng area at the time, told me afterwards that Mao Tse Tung was in the party who fired the shots that July morning. Anyhow, some of the party entered the church, round the time of Communion presumably, because they scattered the Sacred Hosts on the floor and Tim Leonard tried to prevent them physically from desecrating the Blessed Sacrament. The communists stabbed him and took him away and we do not know how long he lived but it does seem that they hacked him to death. The Nanfeng Catholics regarded Tim Leonard as a martyr.

As the fortunes of Chiang Kai Shek and his nationalist army dwindled, inflation sky-rocketed. Over the past year, inflation had already begun to soar. One of the advantages of inflation is that it gives the ordinary man a chance to play at being a millionaire. My chance came in the month of July 1948. I was supplying for Peter Toal in his lovely parish of Kiutu. The teacher who looked after me was called Shih Kuo Thon – we called him Thoni for short. He was very kind and helpful and when I was leaving I gave him a tip of half a million – for the heck of it. I can't remember what the half million would be worth in western currency – about £2.00 or so. But there I was up with the millionaire class.

Back in Nancheng the latest rumour was that the German General, von Paulus, who had been captured by the Russians in the Battle of Stalingrad, was now commanding the Chinese Army north of the Yangtse. It was being said that he was the brains behind the communist advance. In that kind of atmosphere there was a lot of talk, too, of the fact that the famous long march started from Jiangsi Province in 1934. Chiang Kai Shek and his nationalist army were determined to liquidate the embryo Soviet state in Jiangsi. As Chiang intensified his attacks with a vastly superior army, the choice for the communists seemed to be annihilation or retreat. Although the odds were heavily against the communists, they attempted the most amazing retreat in history and it come off. In October 1934, they started the Long March. About 90,000 communist soldiers started to march north from Jianxi. Several thousand others joined on route. During the march, Mao Tse Tung took over and a year later, when they reached Yenan in Shanxi, only 40,000 of them survived the cold, and the military, and aerial bombardments of the Nationalist army who several times thought they had stopped the Reds. The Long March was a triumph for the guerilla tactics of Mao and the determination of the communist soldiers. The Red Army had travelled 7,500 miles.

The older men also reminded us that before the communists started off on the Long March, they had claimed the life of another Columban. His name was Cornelius Tierney and he had been a Clogher priest who was first superior in Nancheng. The communists seized Cornie Tierney on the 14th November, 1930, in a mission station about twenty miles from Nancheng. Cornie had gone out to the mission station to supervise the building of a house for the pastor, John Kerr. It was early morning when the communists seized him and stripped him to the waist in the icy weather. They tied him to a post and flogged him savagely in the presence of the Catholics. Fr Tierney was 59 years of age at the time and nothing was heard of him after the Reds seized him until he smuggled out a personal message to John Kerr, telling the latter where money was hidden and so forth. John Kerr, with great daring and resourcefulness, disguised himself as a coolie and succeeded in going behind the communist lines. He did not, however, manage to see Cornie. When eventually the communists demanded 15,000 U.S. dollars for the safe return of Fr Tierney, communications were so poor that Fr Tierney died before negotiations got under way. He died on February 28th, 1931 and he was regarded as a martyr by the local Catholics.

We reflected that the last time the communists were established in Jiangsi they brought death and martyrdom (hopefully) to two of our Columban missionaries. Now, they were coming again and we wondered what their coming had in store for us. It was a sobering thought.

Soon we had another intimation of the high mortality rate of foreign missionaries in China. During the third week of August, Jerry Buttimer died of heat-stroke in his mission station in Lien Chu. The bishop and about six of us priests took a bus to Nanfeng on our way to the funeral and from there we hired ponies. As we rode along, each of us carried a sun umbrella over our heads, as we were very conscious of the dangers of heat-stroke. Jerry Buttimer was an affable, hard-working missionary and Director of the Nancheng Mission. He was very much missed by his fellow-missionaries and he was loudly mourned by his flock.

CHAPTER 6

Living in Arcadia

Towards the end of August, the bishop tapped me on the shoulder and said, 'I would like to see you, Luke, for a few minutes at 7 o'clock.' When I entered, he was sitting in his chair in his shirt-sleeves, the typewriter on his knees, busy typing out a translation of St Paul's Second Letter to the Corinthians. He worked on it all through the heat of the summer and he needed it for the seminarians. We talked a bit about his translation of the letter and then he told me that the senior seminarians were moving to a place called Kashin as it was considered safe should the Reds quickly cross the Yangtse. The junior seminarians, he told me, were to go to high-school in Linchuan to get their degree. There would be no seminary here for the foreseeable future. 'I am thinking of sending you to the country,' he said. 'Two parishes may be vacant in a couple of weeks. Which do you prefer? Kiutu or Pakan?' When I told him I would go wherever he wanted me to go, he told me that he would like to know my choice because it would help him to make a decision. 'In that case,' I said,'I prefer Pakan because it is newly Christianised and simple instructions will suffice for our Sunday sermons. Kiutu people, on the other hand, are old Catholics and are renowned for their faith and fervour. They need something – well, something more than I feel I can handle now. So I think Pakan would suit me better.' 'Very good,' he said, 'we'll see in a week or two.' In a week or so we did see and I was appointed to Kiutu.

That evening I set out for Kiutu accompanied by Joe Flynn, who came to China a year after me and was still studying the language. He accompanied, or as we would say in Chinese, 'sunged' me to the Wan Nien Chow, which was half way between Nancheng and Kiutu.

Kiutu is ten miles north of Nancheng. At Han Swei Chow you leave the horse path and turn left. Then you can see the solid Gothic church and compound, a little city seated on a hill and ringed around by other hills except on the north side. To the north is a fertile plain stretching as far as the eye can see, covered with patchwork quilts of hundreds of rice fields of most fantastic design and in colour green, gold, bronze and brown according to the season. The valley is watered by a sizeable river which starts as a noisy, frisky little torrent away up in the Mi Wan hills to the west. As it enters the rice valley, it broadens, slows down, and turns gracefully to the east. With excessive dignity and poise for a mere tributary, it continues its journey through miles of rice fields until it enters the Fu, not far from the Wan Nien Chow.

The thing that struck me as most remarkable in this countryside were the stacks of rice straw. The stacks were built on branches of trees or sometimes on the trunk of a tree, at least ten or twelve feet high. The rice sheaves at the bottom seemed to have been tied securely to a branch so as to hold the weight of the stack. The idea was to make sure that the water buffaloes did not get at the rice straw. The people did not have any buffalo-proof sheds. In particular, I noticed a tree growing on the bank of the river. One of its stoutest branches leaned across the river and around this branch was built a straw stack. Sometimes a buffalo would wade body-deep into the river and crane its neck in an effort to get a mouthful of straw. He never quite succeeded but the continued stretching must have added an inch or two to his neck and I have no doubt that in a couple of thousand years the buffaloes of this area will have necks half as long as giraffes' necks.

As I crossed the little bridge that spans the river, a sad-faced, barefooted, middle-aged, middle-sized man in what looked like blue jeans, came hurrying round the corner and shouted when he saw me. 'The priest has come,' he said, 'I intended to meet you at Wan Nien Chow but you got there before me.' His head was closely shaved and his 'blue jeans' were rolled up to his knees. His name was Shong Yung. He was the carrier who helped to carry out messages from Nancheng and other places to the church and compound. Shong Yung and I picked our steps carefully along a beaten path and soon we were in the village. Yu Chia, the home of the Yu tribe as it was called, consisted of two rows of Chinese houses and a cobble stone path running between them. Behind the houses to the south the hills rose sheer and sudden. At the rear of the houses, towards the north, the rice valley fell away to the north-west. 'Sen Fu (Father), we must climb the steps here,' said Shong Yung. About forty stone steps led up to the compound and when we reached the top we were greeted by the Headmaster of the school, Patrick, who smiled graciously and welcomed us with a charming bow. Then came Mr Dong, also a teacher in the school, who was rather shy and blushed deeply as he laughed. He was about the same age as Patrick. Then came Thoni, the little houseboy who was also a teacher. He was only 17, precocious, with a mischievous light in his brown eyes. As I recognised Thoni as the houseboy to whom I had imprudently given a tip of half a million Chinese dollars a month earlier, I was filled with remorse. If I could give him half-a-million before I got a parish, what would he expect now after I had inherited one of the best parishes in the diocese? The three teachers were neatly dressed in Sun Yat Sen suits and they all carried fountain pens in their breast pockets. They were well-educated, refined, Christian gentlemen and a credit to Peter Toal who trained them. Patrick spoke and wrote English pretty well, the others not so well. Mifung, the widow who looked after the orphanage, also came to welcome me. The orphanage was in the village, just outside the compound. It had been purchased by Fr Toal some years previously. Fr Toal had also built the priest's house and it was a substantial house although it had no electricity or running water. All other buildings, church, teacher's house and so forth, were built by the French Vincentians many years before.

The teachers told me that there were about 600 Catholics in the parish, most of them in the village. It was an old Christianity they said, and the first local church was built in 1630. The village tradition was that a Portuguese missionary came to Kiutu in the 17th Century dressed as a merchant. In that disguise he instructed some of the local people and received them into the Church. The first church was destroyed in a persecution by the Taipings (about 1830). The church was re-built by Father Joseph Yu, a native of the village, and it was built out in front of the present teacher's house. The beautiful Camphor tree exuding the lovely odour of camphor, rose on the spot where Father Yu built the second church. (Even now if I close my eyes and see the Kiutu compound and that camphor tree, I can almost sniff the strong scent of the camphor). That church and school and house were burned down in the Boxer Rebellion in

August 1900 and the present church was built by Fr Dellieux, C.M. in 1902. They assured me that my predecessor, Peter Toal, thought that the local Catholics were the best in the whole diocese. They asked me had I realised that in the past two or three generations, there had been five priests by the name of 'Yu'. 'Why does this village have two names?' I asked them. 'You call it Yu Chia and you also call it Kiutu.' Mr Tang explained, 'Yu Chia means the home of the Yu's (the Yu's apparently came from Fujian 400 years earlier) and that is actually the name of this village. Kiutu means the 9th District and it refers to the Civil District in which we live. But seeing the most of our parish is in that District, the church gets its address from the District rather than from the village.'

I soon realised that Kiutu was a very desirable and very well-run parish. It was compact and there were only about three out-missions and they were not very far distant from my house. The teachers and the school were everything one could ask for. It was a delight visiting the children and asking them simple questions from the catechism. Bishop Cleary had composed the catechism we used and it was very simple and clear. To my surprise, I discovered that I loved living on my own and never felt lonely. I had a lot of books, including quite a few of Cardinal Newman's, given to me by a convert in Bristol. I continued to study Chinese and got invaluable help from the three men teachers. I told them to correct me instantly if I made a mistake. Still, preparing the sermon was a heavy chore and one which I took very seriously. I wrote out the sermon in Roman script and then I learned it off by heart. About Friday night, I repeated it for Patrick and asked him to help me; specifically I wanted him to make sure that my pronunciation was the correct one and one that could be understood in the village. I also wanted him to help me with the tones. Patrick was invaluable in helping me to get pronunciations right and in trying to pronounce the tones correctly, and in matters of emphasis.

In the dispensary, where I dispensed pills for malaria and the different fevers and so forth which were prevalent in the area, and where I dressed people's wounds, I heard a language different to the language the teachers spoke. Indeed, Peter Toal felt strongly that I should preach the language, the patois, which the villagers spoke to each other. The teachers, however, tended to speak Mandarin or something which was regarded as a respectable language.

They would not want the priest to preach in the patois. So I had to tell Patrick when I was preparing my sermons to give me pronunciations that the people could understand. After a time I knew instinctively what the people would understand in the matter of doctrine and tried to prepare with that in mind. In the dispensary, I had a chance of learning the people's language and indeed getting to know it well. Medicine was given to everyone who came, whether those who came were believers or not.

Although I loved being on my own, I also loved having company. The priests of the diocese made sure that I did have company. Kiutu was only about 10 miles from Nancheng and when the priests from different parts of the diocese came to visit the Bishop, most of them came to visit me for a night at least. There was always a warm welcome for them but the hospitality, at least according to Western standards, was not great. We did not even have a beer or wine. That is, until Seamus O'Reilly discovered the bonanza. Seamus, a friend from Dalgan days, had a parish south of Nancheng and visited me whenever he could. One day when he was rummaging in a loft in the compound buildings he discovered about twenty bottles of wine in a remote corner. The wine was probably hidden there years earlier when the bandits were visiting the area and subsequently forgotten. Anyhow, finding it was a godsend. Originally it had been Mass wine, but now we had a very big supply of Mass wine recently bought in Shanghai. Over the years it had matured and it added to and enhanced the 'feast of reason' and 'flow of soul' when the priests visited us.

Most of the visitors would just like to sit down after the evening meal and talk and exchange views. Mike Halford, whose parish was twenty miles north of me, and in the north line as we called it, had a more original approach. He would admit ruefully that there were only twelve songs that he sang really well. Then he proceeded to sing them. We would then lapse into conversation. When a lull came in the conversation, he would suggest that we have a bout of speech-making. He would invite me to call him to make a five minute speech without preparation on any subject. Then he would call me to say something informative and inspirational on, say, the Johannine comma or some such subject. (The said comma occurs in St John's First Letter and it's a controversial comma. Some scholars say that it did not exist in the original.) I cannot remember anything about what I said, but I'm certain I didn't go beyond five minutes. The more obscure and the more abstruse the subject the better, according to the rules of this game. It was nearly impossible to stump Mike. The only night I saw him falter for a bit, was when I asked him to kindly say a few well-chosen words on 'Little known aspects of the Pentateuch' (the Pentateuch is the first five books of the Old Testament). Though initially he faltered he soon recovered but I just cannot remember whether he shed any light on the little known aspects of the Pentateuch or not.

What I do remember clearly is the morning, two months later, that Mike's carrier, 'Galloping Hogan', arrived in Kiutu around nine o'clock. He had a short note for me. The note read: 'Come up, Saturn is around.' Mike had quite a good telescope which he had bought from the German Salvatorian Fathers in Shaowu. He was a keen astronomer and I dabbled a fair bit, so I took a day or two off and headed north stopping with Father Luke Teng, the pastor of Pakan, ten miles to the north, for tiffin. Luke Teng and I did the other ten miles to Mike Halford's mission in Kaopi. Pat Sheehy, the pastor of our most northerly mission, Luki, had arrived just before us. Mike Halford showed us round and he was an expert at flowers and trees and shrubs.

When Saturn turned up in due time we looked at the planet through the telescope while Mike monitored the operation and explained to us about the rings round Saturn. All in all we had a hilarious night star-gazing. When our session was finished, Mike reminded us that he expected Jupiter and its moons in the Kaopi skies in due time and that 'Galloping Hogan', on his way to Nancheng on a shopping spree, would alert us as to the day and the hour.

Afterwards we discussed the communist threat and surmised what the communists would do if and when they crossed the Yangtse. By sharing our experiences, each of us acquired a deeper awareness of the problems of the area. The get-together also boosted our morale considerably. It was most interesting to hear Luke Teng summing up the situation as he, a Chinese priest, saw it. He was not very optimistic.

The Sunday after I returned to Kiutu, I gathered from the villagers that Theresa Yu was leaving home to join the Columban Sisters. We escorted her – and when I say we, I mean the whole village, non-believer and Christian alike – to the *ma lu*, the bridle path. She had been a teacher in Lichuan when I was curate there and I knew her well. Her brother, Tommy Yu, was a seminarian and had been sent to continue his studies in Kashin, in southern China. Her sister, Yu Mi Fung, a widow, was in charge of the orphanage. She planned to spend some months with the Columban Sisters in Nancheng and then go to Ireland to do her Novitiate. It was a joyful event in the life of the village.

That November, the Superior General came to visit us. He was Fr Jerry Dennehy, a priest of Nancheng Diocese, who had been elected Superior General a year earlier. He was caught in Ireland when World War II broke out and became a chaplain in the British Forces. Before the war was over he was senior chaplain in the Middle East, I think. He felt very much at home with us and had a conference with Bishop Cleary. Then he took us to the Bishop's oratory and gave us a talk on the current situation. By then it was just a matter of time till the communists would cross the Yangtse and take over South China. He told us that when this happened, he wanted each man to stay at his post. He prayed, he said, and hoped that there would be no loss of life. I was exhilarated by his talk and felt at great peace. He added, of course, that anyone who felt that he should leave was free to do so.

Gerry O'Collins from Hanyang accompanied the Superior General. It was said that Gerry O'Collins was on a secret mission, some thought to Taiwan. He looked the part for such an assignment with the impressive iron grey beard, the sharp penetrating eyes and the cigarette holder from which he smoked continuously. Some of the young men thought that he would be the right man to ask about how we should face up to the new situation, because he had been a prisoner in a Japanese concentration camp during World War II, so I was pushed to ask Gerry a few questions, I said something like this: 'Excuse me Gerry, we're staying here when the Reds come and you have a lot of experience in these matters, so perhaps you could help us. When the time comes, should we queue up for martyrdom in order of seniority, leaving the old men to go first, or should we just queue up higgledy-piggledy?' Gerry was indignant and replied with some feeling, I remember his words exactly, 'I don't want any histrionics. I don't want to go to the Siberian Salt Mines.'

When the Superior General was based in Nancheng he loved to go out to Kiutu to do some shooting. We had wild duck and wild goats in the parish. So I invited him out for a shoot and invited Seamus O'Reilly, too, but he deeply regretted, he said, that he had to rush away. The night before he left, we had a sing-song and Jerry sang, ominously enough, 'The Battle Eve of the Brigade.' I can see him still, a tall, powerfully built man, with the stance of a soldier, his shoulders swaying from side to side as he sang. He appeared to have a lease on life, yet, sad to relate, he was dead in two short years.

The Christmas 1948 Masses were very well attended and the Christmas play was very moving. We had a Mission given by a Chinese priest during the first days of the Chinese New Year. The Retreat boosted the morale of the people and we charged our spiritual batteries. The fruits of the Holy Spirit were very evident amongst the parishioners as far as I could see after the Retreat. The fruits of charity, joy, peace, patience, goodness and so forth. That Christmas and New Year was the happiest, and most peaceful period I remember spending while I was in Kiutu.

There was not a lot of apprehension in Kiutu in the early part of the Spring of 1949. The people in the village felt that China's foreign friends could not, or would not, allow the Reds to conquer China. There were, of course, disturbing rumours all the time but nothing to cause immediate alarm. In Yang Fang, a village about five miles away, and boasting sixty Catholics in a population of five hundred, it was quite a different story. The people there feared and prepared for the worst.

By the middle of April, the Kiutu people got very alarmed as it dawned on them that our foreign friends would not save us from the communists. Lots were cast and two young men were chosen to represent us on the Defence Corps. They were reluctant soldiers and understandably so. Even when the school children sang Nationalist songs exhorting them to deeds of valour as they left the village, the conscripts were anything but eager. Then a few days later the news that the Reds were crossing the Yangtse sent a shock wave through the village. A paralysis seemed to grip the people. All the young men made hasty preparations for flight to the mountains. Anyone who had money or goods of any value sought safe hiding places. When I went into Nancheng, a pall of gloom hung over the countryside. Here and there little groups could be seen talking furtively, terror etched plainly on their faces. Officials from the city, accompanied by Nationalist soldiers, were to be seen in many villages trying to recruit reluctant males. Strangers from the northern part of the province had already arrived in Nancheng and were pushing south before the oncoming Reds could overtake them.

The Bishop and priests were anxious but not tense and their sang-froid was reassuring. Bishop Cleary was preparing a circular letter to send to his priests. I quote from it: 'There's to be no rushing into Nancheng, no matter what happens. Each priest is to meet the communists at the door of his church or compound. If, for some reason or other, a priest has to leave his church or hide, let him hide within the parish.' He gave us strong, clear and intelligent leadership.

Towards the end of April, Wang Bay Hua rushed into the room where I was having my evening meal. 'Did you hear,' he said, 'that the Reds have shelled a British gunboat on the Yangste, killing a number of the crew.' 'I don't believe it,' I said, 'they wouldn't dare to fire at a British boat. If by chance such a thing did happen then the odds are that it would bring Britain into the war against the Reds. If the British come in it looks as if America will come in too.' When the gunboat story was confirmed, and we learned that the gunboat was the HMS Amethyst, hopes soared for a day or two, but soon it became evident that the British would not retaliate.

And then, early in May, one evening Thoni came running in, hardly able to speak in his excitement. 'The Reds are marching on Nanchang, the Capital of this province. They are only fifty miles from here. Alas, alas! Maybe you should go to Nancheng and stay there with the rest of the priests.' 'No,' I replied, 'I stay here.'

On the 7th May, 1949, Nanchang fell to the Red Generals Lin Biao and Liu Pu Shin. That day, the Nationalist representative from Kiutu came in to discuss current affairs with me. It was Wang Bay Hua and his face was heavy with worry. 'This is the end,' he said, 'they will certainly shoot me. It is too late to fly. They robbed us in 1931 and destroyed our house, now they will destroy me.' Poor Bay Hua, as we called him. As a child he saw his parents lose all their property when the communists came to Jiangsi. Now, in his forties, with five children of his own, he saw the dreaded communists coming back and he expected no mercy. He was a charming gentleman, an excellent Catholic and an ordinary farmer. Though his forebodings were well-founded, he could not console himself with the consideration that it would take the communists a long time to get established locally. And then there was always hope, faint though it might seem just then, that the Nationalists would return and pulverise the communist armies now that they had crossed the Yangtse.

PART II:

The Persecution

CHAPTER 7

Run for Cover

There is a Chinese proverb which goes, 'Of all the thirty-six options available, running away is the best'. The proverb always intrigued and amused me. But, mind you, when the bandits came, I began to see that it contained a layer of hidden wisdom too.

The bandits came in the wake of the Red Army and the Red Army came very unexpectedly to our district on May 9th 1949. That afternoon, I had walked to an outlying mission station some miles away to baptise a baby. On my return journey, as I approached the bridle path, I could scarcely believe my eyes. Yes, there they were, the advance guard of the communist Army marching into South China and into history. The soldiers were unchallenged, marching along casually in groups of twenty or thirty, the groups following each other at intervals of 150 yards. They sang a communist song, 'Mei Yu Chung San Tang, Mei Yu Shin Dzung Kuo', 'No Communist Party, No New China'. But they were an army in a hurry.

I slipped across the bridle path between two detachments and, unlike Lot's wife, never looked back till I reached the church compound. They left only a token garrison in the county capital. They made no attempt to organise local government in the countryside. The result was that gangs of bandits suddenly sprang up like mushrooms after a rainy night in July, all over the district. some of the bandits were deserters from the Nationalist Army which had fled before the advancing Reds, others were civilians who had been misled into joining a gang.

Their methods were simple. They called on people who were supposed to be well off and asked for money or other valuables. If the people pleaded poverty, as they usually did, the bandits singed their skin with burning faggots, or hung them up by their thumbs, or even held one of their children for ransom.

None of the Chinese in my village stayed home at night while the bandits were on the prowl. Each evening, Christians and non-believers alike took to the hills with as much of their goods and chattels as they could carry. At dawn, they returned to the village, because the bandits had an unwritten law that they finished their operations well before daybreak.

For the first week, I turned a deaf ear to the entreaties of the Christians that I should take to the 'everlasting hills' each night with my flock. However, the realistic argument of a hard-headed merchant at length prevailed. 'How much money have you in the house?' 'About five dollars,' I replied. A look of terror came into his eyes. 'Do you think that the bandits will believe you if you tell them that? They are convinced every foreign priest is well off and that the Bishop would pay a couple of thousand dollars ransom money for your release.' He spoke slowly and with great conviction.

His words jolted me – no bishop in his senses, I felt, could afford the outrageous extravagance of paying a couple of thousand dollars ransom for me. I know only too well that my Bishop was in his senses round the clock so I decided that, of all the options, and there were far less than thirty-six of them, running away to the hills was the one for me.

The prospect of going on the run brought me a sense of boyish adventure. But first there was the problem of leaving my house in a proper state of preparedness for the bandits. The Chinese, with 4,000 years of civilisation behind them, have a ritual for this eventuality.

The approach was spelled out for me by the hard-headed merchant. 'Leave the door open,' he said. 'That doesn't sound very wise,' I replied. 'Well,' he continued, more in sorrow than in anger at my European obtuseness, 'if you lock it the bandits will break it down and then you will have no door. You have a small safe there,' he went on, 'leave it open and leave the dollars where they can easily find them. This will give the bandits a bit of "face". As well as that, it will keep them from getting annoyed. If they get annoyed at what they regard as a discourtesy, they would resort to extreme measures like burning down your house.' Burning down my house, I mused, is a bit much, but breaking down the door on top of that is the limit, even for a bandit. But my instructions were not yet complete. 'Take your own clothes out of the house,' he said, 'and hide them somewhere else. Then leave used garments and shoes as a gesture of goodwill for the bandits.'

That evening, Mr Dong and I were busy preparing to go on the run. We hid my clothes in so many different places that, afterwards, we forgot where some items were hidden. My predecessor had gone on leave and, to keep the bandits happy, I left out for them his best Chinese gown and his best foreign clothes – woollen cap, umbrella and so forth. As sundown approached, I noted with satisfaction that we had carried out, in detail, the instructions given by the merchant. I noted with less satisfaction that Mr Dong was getting more serious and silent as we finished our preparations. To boost his morale a bit, I ventured, 'Mr Dong, do you think we should leave a note for the bandits saying we regret we have been called to the hills on urgent business and cannot be on hand to receive them?' The gravity lifted and he laughed heartily as he replied, 'No need for a note. I think the bandits will understand.'

In fairness to Mr Dong, there were good grounds for gravity. The hills to which we were fleeing were pretty well jungle, inhabited by snakes, who came in different sizes and species. Other habitants were tigers who had the audacity to come down to the village from time to time and help themselves to village pigs and, of course, mosquitoes were there in droves. Mr Dong detested tigers, while I had little time for snakes. Their bite was much worse than their bark!

We were fortunate, though, because with Mr Dong's expert guidance, we wended our way cautiously through briars, brushwood and brambles without encountering any of our 'kindred of the wild'. In about an hour, we reached a fairly bare hilltop. From our vantage point, we could see the occasional flicker from the bandits' torches in the spacious valley below. According to Mr Dong, they were heading for a village on the other side of the valley remote from us – so we just waited wearily, beating off the ever-present mosquitoes with fans till the first flush of dawn drove the bandits from the valley. Then we returned to church and I said Mass with quite a large congregation present.

Next day, the Columban Sisters at Headquarters kindly sent me a pair of dungarees. In a note, Sr Attracta, the Nursing Sister, said the ordinary snake bite would not penetrate through the hard material from which the dungarees were made. The threat from the snakes receded; I had the ultimate deterrent. So I went on the run relatively carefree till the next note from the Columban Sisters arrived a few days later. The gist of it was that if a snake were biting really well and in good form, then he could penetrate through the dungarees and I would find myself suffering from snake bite. In which case, all I had to do was simply bleed the vein between the snake bite and the heart, making sure that I had used a sterilised razor blade, then apply a tourniquet and, presumably, live happily ever afterwards.

The rigmarole about the tourniquet, I heard before when we did a crash course on tropical medicine in University College, Dublin, as seminarians. But putting it into practice, with the possibility of a tiger looking over one's shoulder and the certainty of a swarm of mosquitoes ready and willing to sting a debilitating dose of malaria into one's system, was a fairly sticky problem. No longer carefree, I pondered on the problem as we climbed the hills and, later that night, I got a severe dose of fatalism, compounded with fantasy. This was the night, I felt sure, a snake would bite me right through the dungarees. As we could not turn on a torch without attracting the attention of the bandits, the odds were that I would mess up the tourniquet and razor blade operation and bleed to death. Strange to say, the prospect of death did not worry me much, because I doubt if I shall ever be as well prepared again as during those hectic and sometimes hilarious days. But the dreaded snake didn't turn up that night, and neither did the bandits.

I was getting rather tired of all this waiting around, what with five or six nights on the hills and attending to people who came to the dispensary during the day, so I decided to go to a Mission Station about seven miles away and say Mass for the people and have a good sleep. Once the Reds got established, they might not allow me to go. Mr Dong was less than enthusiastic and did not consider my idea particularly bright.

Maybe he sensed that I was running away from my problem, which I was, and that I might run into another, which I did. However, he did admit that Yang Fang village was a rather remote place, unlikely to attract bandits and that it would afford us an opportunity of catching up on our sleep. So we sent word to Li Tai

Li, in whose house we usually had Mass, and toddled off on our journey under a roasting sun of a morning in June. We walked briskly for an hour and rested for a few minutes at a Catholic's house in the village of Wu ti tien. To our consternation, we learned that Wu ti tien had been raided by bandits the night before. The people were still scared. And talk about rumours! I don't like boasting, but I think this part of my parish must have been one of the most prolific rumour-producing belts in China. Blood curdling, terror inspiring, original, plausible rumours. Usually garnished with the genuine gestures the bandits used and the words they said before punishing their victims, real or imaginary.

Thus encouraged, we set off on the second leg of our journey and reached Yang Fang shortly after high noon. Li Tai Li received us cordially. We had a wash, a change and then a nice meal. During the meal somebody mentioned that a tiger had come down from the hills the night before and carried off a calf. I was shown to my large room, one end of which was the buffalo's apartment. As it happened, he was out that afternoon and I fell into a deep overdue sleep as soon as I lay on the bamboo bed.

A few hours later, I woke to find the village humming with excitement. Reliable information had reached Yang Fang that the bandits were coming there that very night. When I got up, everybody was preparing for the hills. Blankets and clothes were folded up and put into boxes and a constant stream of basket carriers operated between the village and the hideout on the hilltop a mile away. All valuables, everything in fact which might place temptation in the way of a bandit, were either buried underground or taken to the hills. Old pigs were driven and also cattle. As pastor, I felt I should lend a willing hand, now making a flying tackle on a fleeing pig, now grabbing a chicken in flight. By nightfall, Yang Fang was deserted.

The site chosen for our bivouac commanded a good view of the village and the valley beneath but we were quite invisible from either. Li Tai Li very kindly brought out a door for me to sleep on and laid it by the side of a stream. He placed a smouldering dried plant near my head and said the smoke would keep the mosquitoes at bay. We said the Rosary in whispers as did all the Catholics who lay on their mats along the hillside. I was just dozing off on the door when

Mr Dong called me in a frightened whisper, 'Sen Fu,' he said, 'I am very scared.' 'What are you scared about?' I replied a little testily I fear, and his fright was very understandable. 'You remember,' he continued, 'the tiger who came to Yang Fang and ate the calf, it was from this hill that he came.' Well, it was not the most tranquilising bedtime thought and for a little time after that I couldn't get off to sleep but I did have the opportunity of hearing the frogs serenade in the neighbouring ponds. They seemed to be striking up a sprightly tune, as if piping out the bandits. Maybe they don't make music in the strict sense of the word. Maybe outside the scale, there is none. But they seemed quite melodious just then. They say the ear is not filled with hearing but the sounds of a summer night in tropical China make a good attempt. I wonder did anyone ever count them. There were old frogs, who had borne the burden of the day, with weak voices. Then the cicada with its whank, whank, whank, like the sound one makes when sharpening a scythe with a stone. And then cicadas in low gear who emit a kind of purring sound. And then the night bird (I am told) with a sort of whistle. All in harmony, all orchestrating with other birds in the country-side, all serenading the Creator. And so to sleep.

About two hours later, I was awakened by a whisper saying the bandits had come. I saw the faint glimmer of a torch in the foothills to the east of us. They were making for the village. When you have a door for a bedroom, it is child's play to convert it into a bedsitter. I invited Mr Dong to come and sit beside me. 'I wonder what they will do,' he said. 'They are bound to be upset when they reach the village and find all the property and all the people gone.' 'Yes,' I said, 'they are rather sensitive on points like that.' Nearer and near-er came the bandits. We waited in suspense. The cry of a child, the mooing of a cow, the grunt of a pig might betray us. The shadowy figures crouched low as they approached the village. 'They are just opposite us,' whispered Mr Dong, 'not 200 yards away.' 'They are past us,' he explained joyously, 'thanks be to God.'

When the bandits discovered that the property and people of Yang Fang had disappeared without trace, they were disappointed and rather irritated. To show their displeasure, they broke a few benches, and continued their journey westward. Soon, I was wakened by Li Tai Li's shout 'Pan shin gung,' a new and beautiful day had dawned. 'Pan shin gung' means 'make your confessions' and Li Tai

Li was just reminding the people that confessions would be heard before Mass. The people on the hillside had already started for the village. Like the snail who carries his house on his head, I picked up my bedsitter and took my place in the procession.

In a few minutes, the Catholics were making their confessions. Before starting Mass, we noticed that quite a number of non-believers were present. They felt that they had a lot to be thankful for, but they did not know whom to thank. I told them in the homily that Eucharist literally means thanksgiving and that, united with Our Lord in the Mass, we were able to give worthy thanks to God, who had brought us safely through the 'terrors of the night'.

It was a moving and memorable ceremony and the Christians sang the prayers in Chinese soulfully and from the heart. It was the last Mass in Yang Fang.

I Sabotage the Revolution

All through the month of June there were rumours, most of them based on wishful thinking, that the Americans would attack from Taiwan. There were also rumours that the Nationalists would stage a counter-attack from remote hideouts in southern China. We knew, of course, that there were small groups of retreating Nationalists making their way south all the time. About three times retreating Nationalist soldiers stayed in an old seminary in our parish. The old seminary, which some years earlier Bishop Cleary had given to poor people in the locality as a dwelling place, was about three-quarters of a mile from the church. Each time when we heard that the Nationalists had taken up residence for a day or two in the seminary I asked them to kindly leave as we would be charged with harbouring them when the Reds got established. Each time they promised they would leave at once, but they did not keep their promises. That is how I 'sabotaged the Red Revolution' and made it to the top of the communist crime chart.

The only time I have had a meteoric rise in my career was when the communists launched me into the world of crime. I discovered that a meteoric rise can bring headaches and dizziness, but it was the parishioners rather than I who suffered most from the headaches. They were deeply distressed when they heard I was charged with sabotage and I think they realised that I didn't understand the full implications of the charge. With their traditional good manners and tract, they informed me that sabotaging the Revolution in a communist country wasn't a recipe for longevity. When I protested that I did not commit the crime of sabotage but that the Reds just labelled me with that crime, I was told that as far as the communist justice was concerned the label was sufficient to convict me. The penalty fits the label.

Locally, there was swift reaction when the communists got established in our area. Pat Sheehy, thirty miles north of my mission, stayed a night with me on his way to the Bishop's residence in Nancheng. We were having breakfast next morning at 6 a.m. as he wanted to be on the road before it got too hot. Suddenly, the door of the house was pushed open and in rushed an officer of the Red Army. He covered us with his revolver and shouted, 'Where are the bandits?' I said, 'What bandits?' and indicated that I was the priest in charge. Then he saw Pat Sheehy's carrier Lao Dzung come into the room and he covered him with his revolver and screamed at him. 'You are a bandit.' The carrier calmly produced his travel pass and said he did not belong to our county and stated that he was not a bandit.

The officer said angrily that I had harboured, entertained and given red carpet treatment to bandits who had stayed in the old seminary some weeks back. It was his opinion, he continued, that I was still harbouring bandits and therefore he must make a careful search. He searched the house from the foundation stone to the chimney pots and the orphanage and the church and the school. He found no bandits but warned me that justice would be meted out to me in due time by the People's Army of Liberation. Shortly afterwards the communists closed down our Catholic schools in case, they said, bandits might seek shelter there. It seemed a high-handed and vindictive act and it caused us great distress in the parish.

In Nancheng, the capital of the county, there was reaction too. The authorities there held the Bishop responsible for my crimes, they said. Accordingly, the Bishop's Administrator, Barney O'Neill, was called down to a Commissar's office and excoriated on account of my crimes. The Commissar was truculent, menacing and furious. Whenever my name was mentioned he seemed to be threatened with apoplexy. After a stormy session he told Barney that I must come to Nancheng within three days and that I must give him a written and abject apology for sabotaging the Red Revolution.

On my way to Nancheng, I was going along the bridal path when suddenly I heard the command, 'Shen Shou', 'hands up', barked at me from behind some clumps of bushes on both sides of the path. I raised my hands and an officer of the Liberation Army came forward from either side covering me with their rifles as they came. I thought the spokesman was just that little bit cynical when he said,

'I suppose you're going to meet bandits somewhere.' 'No,' I said, 'as a matter of fact I have been invited by the Commissar to Nancheng.' Of course he knew well where I was going because he called me a criminal and pointed out that sabotaging the revolution was a dastardly crime, crying to Mao Tse Tung for vengeance. Abruptly he stopped lecturing me, stared at me with a murderous scowl and asked, 'Are you carrying any guns or bombs?' 'No,' I replied. 'Search him,' he roared to the other officer. The latter searched me and reported, 'He has no arms - no lethal weapons of any kind.' 'Go on,' roared the spokesman, still covering me with a rifle and a murderous scowl. The object of the exercise was to terrify me. The hatred in the face of that officer haunted me for the rest of the journey. Mao Tse Tung has written that all 'politics flow from the mouth of a gun'. I had met members of the People's Army of Liberation only twice as yet, but each time they communicated with me along the barrel of a gun. The gun, I learned, is a very effective instrument of communication.

At the Bishop's house in Nancheng, I found them calm but apprehensive. The Bishop said I should give the Reds an apology, saying I was only a couple of years in the country and that my ignorance of Chinese customs and my imperfect knowledge of the Chinese language was responsible for any mistake I may have made. 'As a matter of fact,' he said, with a mischievous laugh, 'I have written out an apology for you and it is now being translated into diplomatic Chinese. You remember St Paul's admonition to Timothy, 'Let no man despise thee for thy youth'? Now I am hoping that this apology will make the Reds realise that your youth and inexperience was responsible for what they call your crimes. Let them despise you for your youth. I think this is our only hope of keeping you out of jail.'

The next day Barney O'Neill took the apology to the county Commissar at 5.00 p.m. They humiliated him, keeping him waiting for an hour. When he was admitted to the office he was told the Commissar was out of town. The Deputy who dealt with Barney was much more truculent and obnoxious than the Commissar himself. When he read my apology he flew into a rage and said he did not believe a word of it. He threw it back to Barney and said he wanted the name and address of every bandit who stayed in the old seminary and the duration of their stay. When Barney said this was impossible, the Deputy started to shout at him and to repeat the same old charges again and again. Eventually, after two and a half hours, Barney was told that the Commissar would be back at 5.00 p.m. on Thursday and that he should come again with a new apology and the names and addresses of the bandits.

I was feeling rather tense after Barney was gone for two hours and there was no sign of him returning. Everybody else was tense too because this was our first encounter with the communist authority at the county level. The bishop came down the stairs after Barney had gone about an hour, peeped over his glasses and asked us anxiously, 'Is there any sign of Barney?' Tom Fisher, Joe Flynn and I and somebody else, started to play a game of bridge, but we could not concentrate. The tall French grandfather clock had always been there in the hall but that night I seemed to hear it for the first time. It seemed to boom out each quarter with slow, laboured beats as if each was going to be its last. Barney returned after about three hours and looked a pale, sickly green, but there was anger and resentment in his face too. He took off his sun helmet and after he wiped his forehead and shook his head a few times, he muttered, 'These Reds.' Then he told us his story and when Bishop Cleary heard it, he remarked, 'We can make the apology more abstract and abject. Regarding the bandits, everyone knows the names like Feng Yi Chi. We can say we heard he was there (which we did) and this will give them a little face and maybe pacify them.' 'I'm sick and tired of it,' replied Barney, 'and it looks anything but hopeful.' This was the first I heard of the communists expecting me to give them the names of the bandits. Surely they could not expect me to go to the bandits and say 'I have a visitor's book and I should be grateful if you would sign your names and addresses in the book and leave a forwarding address in case you are urgently needed'? Bandits would not stand for such an intrusion into their privacy as I knew well from my experience.

On the Thursday, the Commissar was in a better mood. He accepted the apology. He repeated that were it not for the mercy of the People's Army of Liberation, I should be in jail long since. Barney assured him that far from entertaining bandits, I feared them. Barney asserted that I would be afraid to go back to the parish even now if I were allowed to go back. This was a good, an excellent psychological thrust and it enraged the County Commissar. 'The foreigner afraid of the bandits,' he said, 'even after the Red Army have liberated the Chinese?' Both he and his deputy laughed loudly and cynically. 'Then,' continued the Commissar, 'the foreigner may return to the country tomorrow. But don't think the case is finished. The authorities will continue the investigation in Kiutu.'

The news was received with joy at the Bishop's house. Now that things looked a little more hopeful, Joe Flynn suggested I should be presented to the County Commissar in person. Barney O'Neill was not enthusiastic but he said he would ask our catechist, John McCormack, for his opinion. (John McCormach was so nick-named because of his beautiful voice and his fondness of the McCormack songs we sang.) The latter would not hear of it. The reason was, he said, that in the apology I stated that my mistake was due to my youth and inexperience. 'Youth,' he said, 'when in the eyes of the Chinese he looks ages older than he did before the Reds came? Don't take him to the commissar.'

It was with mixed feelings I started back, full of gratitude that I was able to return to help my people and that I was not in jail. Full of misgivings, too, as to what extent I would be allowed to function as a priest. How to live out my role as pastor while trying to live down the role of criminal in which the communists had cast me, that was the problem always recurring.

It was a dark morning for July and whenever I think of my journey back to Kiutu Arthur Koestler's book 'Darkness at Noon' comes to mind. The book is about Russia under Stalin in the thirties. Specifically it is about the generals who were forced to confess to crimes they never committed and had been liquidated by Stalin. Why I should think of that book I do not know but that is the way association of ideas works in my mind. The light of freedom as we understood it had been snuffed out. The countryside seemed strangely dark and subdued with few people on the road. But I could not allow sombre thoughts of that nature to occupy my mind for too long. The Chinese have a proverb which says, 'You cannot keep the bird of sorrow from flying over your head, but you can prevent it from nesting in your hair.' The bird of sorrow was flying pretty low that day alright, but the way I kept him out of my hair was to look back on other trips I had made from Nancheng to Kiutu, especially the one I made on board the Mongolian mule, about a year earlier.

As I entered the church compound, there were two communist officers standing, one each side of the gate. They seemed to ignore me but one of them said to the other in a fairly loud voice which was obviously meant for me, 'Did we not shoot that foreign imperialist yet? I thought we had shot him.' This time they were communicating to me not along the barrel of a gun but in a much more effective and subtle manner. They were communicating to me, unofficially, the Party thinking. Unfortunately, Patrick, who had been headmaster until the Reds closed down our school, heard them as he came out to meet me and he was terrified. Patrick was a neat phrasemaker and he summarised the situation in the words 'Hen wei shin', meaning 'very dangerous', but living dangerously has compensations. It is never boring and the adrenalin flows fairly fast.

That night in the silence of my house in Kiutu, I reflected on the events of the past week since I had been summoned to Nancheng. It had been said that the Reds, even before they crossed the Yangtse, had got a 'new look'. It had been said that they were no longer killing priests or persecuting Christians but according to Columban Ted MacElroy, in areas occupied by the Reds from 1945 to 1948, 57 Catholic priests, including foreigners, had been killed. Some were shot, some were beaten or burnt to death, some dragged along by horses until they died. The picture of that Red officer's face with the murderous scowl on it, who stopped me on my way to Nancheng, came back to my mind that night. I was on my own now in the quietness of the night and I wondered was the so-called 'new look' a reality or was it just a propaganda gesture. From my experience, I felt that the killing of priests might yet be on the communist agenda.

Back in the parish next morning very early, Red Army bugles could be heard in the hillsides surrounding the village. Their objectives were to establish local Government in the area, capture remnants of Nationalist forces and to invite the people to a General Assembly. As soon as the people heard that the Reds were coming to the area in force, every man in the village, from sixteen to nearly sixty, fled at full speed away from the soldiers, up the steps leading to the church and onto the hills where they hid. My reaction to this was one of pleasant surprise to note that I had such promising athletes in the parish. If you saw some of those fairly old men and the spurt of speed they put up, you would not say that the Chinese were a lethargic race. Hot on their heels came the soldiers, up the steps.

They were surprised to find that our church was at the top of the steps and I think they were very surprised to find two teachers, Mr Dong and Thoni, and myself standing in the church porch looking highly amused and discussing the flight of our fellow villagers. 'Where have you hidden them? To where have they gone?' snapped the soldiers angrily. 'We do not know,' we replied. We had a difficult time convincing the soldiers that we had not hidden the villagers. Loyalty to one's fellow-villagers was quite a virtue with the Chinese.

That night the Red scouts camped on the hillside that overlooked our house, hoping that they might intercept some of the villagers who had fled to the hills that morning. Thoni was alarmed. 'The Reds could shoot us through the windows at night from that hillside,' he said. 'They hate us so much. Perhaps it is better for us not to sleep here.' I had great sympathy for him, but I had to stay in the house. So we doubled up some Pee Wos, padded Chinese blankets like continental quilts but much thicker. We placed them on the inside of the windows facing the hillside and I felt sure that the Pee Wos would stop bullets. But they did not shoot at us that night.

The school year would soon be starting again and, as pastor, I had to see that the children were taught about their faith. Now that the Reds has closed our own school, what we did was to ask the parents if the children could come to the church, each day after school, for half an hour, so that we could teach them about their religion. To this, the parents readily agreed and the arrangement worked well for some time. The communists also forbade me to pay pastoral visits to the Catholic homes in the village. I think the reason they gave was that such visits would be used by me to make contact with Nationalist guerillas or bandits. The prohibition, they said, was in the interests of good order and national security. We got round this with the help of two praesidia of the Legion of Mary which I started shortly after I came to the parish, a senior praesidium and a junior praesidium for the boys. Later we started a junior praesidium for the girls.

We had to hold our Legion meetings secretly because, to put it mildly, the Reds frowned on the Legion. We held the weekly meetings in the sacristy. During the meetings, Thoni kept watch from the top of the steps that led up to the church. Whenever he saw the

Reds approaching, he rushed into the sacristy to warn us. The look-out man was a feature of the Catholic resistance in Ireland during penal times and maybe that's how I got the idea.

Then the meeting would disband as follows. The legionaries (seven ladies and a man, we had in the senior praesidium), would go into the church and some would say their prayers privately and others would do a lot of dusting or cleaning. Some might go out and collect firewood in the nearby hill. My part was to leave the sacristy through the door that led to the priest's house, welcome the communists and engage them in lively conversation; nothing very original or profound. For starters, we would have an exchange of bows, then I put them two customary questions, 'Have you eaten rice?' and secondly, 'Have you eaten to repletion?' Then an exchange of platitudes would take place and eventually they would say that they wanted some medicine for malaria or whatever.

Despite the interruptions, we continued our legionary meetings and at the meetings I assigned to the legionaries the work they were to do during the next week. In this way they visited the families I would like to have visited. Of the seven members of our senior praesidium, only one – Thoni's father – wrote Chinese characters. So I appointed him secretary. Mike Halford was suitably impressed and he said it was the most brilliant decision he had ever seen me make. Of course, other members of the praesidium wrote some characters, but he wrote a large number and wrote them fluently. They were most zealous, though all of them except two were sixty years old, I never knew them to omit the weekly two-hour apostolic work, even when the weather was unfavourable. I too was enriched by listening to them report on their work each week. The danger for the missionary who has just started preaching in Chinese is that he will use exhortations and illustrations which he would use in Europe. I discovered that the illustrations they used, the examples and the exhortations they gave, were typically Chinese and calculated to influence their listeners. So I shamelessly copied the examples, the illustrations and the type of exhortations they gave when preaching myself.

God blessed the pastoral work done by the legionaries by bringing back some of the lapsed and by encouraging the practising Catholics to become more fervent and deeply Christian. We had also two junior praesidia, one for the boys and one for the girls. The ages ranged from 11 to 14 or thereabouts. The boys taught their young brothers who had not yet started school the simple questions of the catechism and the ordinary prayers. The girls did the same for their younger sisters and for other relatives. Parents were frequently out at meetings organised by the Reds.

We were satisfied enough with the measures we had taken to counteract the onslaught on freedom of religion made by the communists in our parish. The Reds made sure they wouldn't let me forget that they had declared me a criminal. Even when they came to the dispensary that Autumn of 1949, they would mention casually that I was the priest who had sabotaged the Revolution. They seemed to insinuate that the survival rate amongst saboteurs of the Revolution was exceedingly low. It seemed then that once they had declared me a criminal, the stigma would stay with me, a heavy weight round my neck like the albatross round the neck of the 'Ancient Mariner' in the poem of that name.

When living dangerously becomes your lifestyle, surviving one danger in time to grapple with the next can become very invigorating. For me, a change of trouble became a bit of a break. But for us missionaries, the big break came when the communist Constitution was published in October 1949. It guaranteed freedom of religion. The local communist authorities visited me and assured me that they were sincere when they guaranteed freedom of religion. It was their duty to see that the Constitution would be upheld all over China. Many Catholics and priests believed that the Chinese communists had got not merely a 'new look' but a change of heart. As they were now the de facto government of China, they would be seeking recognition from the United Nations. If they denied us freedom of religion, there would not be much hope of getting recognition. In fairness to the local communists, they seemed to be less repressive after the Constitution was formulated, so I decided to travel into Nancheng.

In contrast to my last journey to Nancheng a few months earlier, this one was a pleasant experience. Not only were there no guns pointed at me, or no murderous scowls thrown in my direction, there wasn't any soldier in sight as far as I could see. The light of freedom seemed to be switched on again. Quite a few of the priests of the Diocese had come in to headquarters, and headquarters was full of hope and cheer and hilarity. According to Bishop Cleary, the bishops of our Province were of the opinion that we might be able to co-exist with Communism. They did not expect we would have full freedom of religion. Most of the priests present concurred with the opinion of the bishops. If a pastor did not have any trouble with the communists in his parish before October 1949, then he continued to be cautiously hopeful. I was practically the only priest who had got into serious trouble with the Reds and, as a result of it, I got a lot of good-natured ribbing from my fellow priests at headquarters. A close friend of mine said that the Reds were pretty shrewd and that they had seen through me in double-quick time.

Though we differed on our views of the Church's chances under Communism, getting together was a great boost to our morale because most of the parishes in our Diocese were manned by just one young priest. Meeting my fellow priests had a therapeutic effect on me personally. The liveliness, the laughter, the high spirits were so infectious that I wondered if I had not been too gloomy in my assessment of the situation. I wondered if my problem was not a persecution complex after all – and that is a mental disorder. So I decided to have another bash at reading the signs of the times when I returned to Kiutu.

CHAPTER 9

The Pastor in Persecution

Reading the signs of the times when you are dealing with communists is not an easy exercise, as Winston Churchill discovered. When asked about a meeting with Stalin from which he had returned, he is reported to have said, 'Stalin is an enigma, wrapped up in a mystery, inside a conundrum.' I would say much the same about my meetings with the local communist leaders.

An official who visited me declared that the Communist Constitution gave us freedom of religion, and that the Constitution would be upheld even in remote villages like ours. Then that same official addressed the villagers, most of whom were Catholics, and repeated the declaration. As an afterthought, he said, mockingly, 'You believe in God. Have you seen him? You believe in the soul. Have you seen the soul go up to heaven?' Then he and his staff laughed loudly and cynically at the idea of religion, and at the gullibility of people who had religious beliefs. The Catholics were upset and felt threatened. The 'double speak' of the official was calculated to mystify us and to confuse us regarding what he meant by freedom of religion. That is exactly the effect it did have.

So, if I was unable to read the signs of the times from what the communists said to me, I must judge their intentions from what they did since they came to our district and what they would do in the coming months.

By the Spring of 1950, I felt in my bones that persecution was imminent. What to do till the persecution actually strikes was the question to which I addressed myself in the early summer of that year. I found I had little experience of being a pastor and knew nothing about persecution but I was at that age of incredible innocence when I thought that books, especially theology books etc., had the answers to any problems the pastor might encounter. What I was looking for was a slim volume with something like 'The Busy Pas-

tor's Guide to Persecution' for its title. To my great disappointment, the load of theology books I had lugged across the planet,
were silent on the subject. My Church History manual was far from
silent. In fact, it gave a list of persecutions complete with dates and
durations from the first century onwards. But it gave no practical
lessons from other centuries which might help a twentieth-century
pastor with a persecution coming up in his parish. In my uncharita-
bleness, I wondered if the authors of Church History manuals were
not a little like the Bourbon Kings, who, it is said, never forgot anything and never learned anything.

Then, in my frustration, I reached out for the Bible, and opened it
instinctively at the last volume in the New Testament – The Book of
Revelation we call it now, The Apocalypse we called it then. From
my reading, I gathered that the author had witnessed during persecution himself, and at the time of writing he was doing hard-labour
in the quarries of Patmos, because of the witness he bore. The Book
of Revelation was written for Christian communities in Western
Asia who were being persecuted for their faith towards the end of
the first century. Its aim was to give them encouragement and
hope. It was saying to them that persecutions pass and that victory
in Christ lies ahead for the persecuted who witness, suffer and persevere. It was giving to us, a Christian community in Eastern Asia
in the twentieth century, a similar message of steadfast trust in the
Risen Lord of all peoples. It urges each new Christian community
to 'listen to what the Spirit is saying to the church (of today)' (Rev
2:7,11,16,ff). The Book of Revelation is resistance literature for the
persecuted in every century. It is the busy pastor's guide to persecution.

Some months before I started to read the Book of Revelation, I had
borrowed 'St John and the Apocalypse' by Father Martindale, S.J.,
from Bishop Cleary's library in Nancheng. Was borrowing the
book an instinctive action or was it a case of 'future events casting
their shadows before'? I do not know. Martindale's commentary is
not a verse-by-verse one, but it does give a picture of the book's
structure and its message as he saw them. In his analysis of persecution in the early church, he notes that unofficial persecutions can
be more severe and damaging than official ones. That thought-
provoking sentence set me thinking. Although the distinction was
new to me, I soon realised the truth of Martindale's statement. If an

official persecution is declared, the pastor can prepare his people and himself so that all are spiritually braced to meet it. The unofficial persecution may be taking place before his eyes. He is lulled into a false sense of security and then one day he discovers that the local Church is being undermined and he blames himself for lack of judgement.

Thanks to the commentary, I woke up to the fact that an unofficial persecution had been taking place in Kiutu almost since the Red takeover a year and a half earlier. Incidents which I had regarded as isolated acts of religious repression, I now saw as part of a planned build-up to a large-scale persecution. One of the incidents concerned a girl called Shay Yung. She was about eighteen, a native of the parish and she belonged to an old Catholic family. The Reds ordered her to attend a training course on communist ideology because she was a bright girl. The course took place in a college in a town a hundred miles from Nancheng. On the last night of the course, two women in Shay Yung's dormitory were detailed to force her to renounce her faith. Shay Yung protested that the freedom to believe in God as her ancestors had done for generations was her constitutional right. 'Belief in God is a foreign superstition,' they shouted, 'and this business about your ancestors is outmoded Confucianism from which Chairman Mao has liberated us. If you don't apostatise and throw away that crucifix you are wearing, we won't let you sleep tonight.' Then all of the twenty women in the dormitory continued to intimidate poor Shay Yung. This was part of the plan. 'Cannot you apostatise and let us go to sleep?' they kept shouting all night long. Towards the dawn, the women, pretty well hysterical, screamed at Shay Yung urging her to apostatise but she held out. Sad to relate the next time the Reds repeated this 'blitzkrieg' type of psychological torture, Shay Yung succumbed and renounced her faith. But that was not the end of it. Some time later, Tai Yang, another parishioner, was sent to do the same course. She was a convert and had been received into the Church before she married. Her husband was a lukewarm Catholic. On the last night of the course, the women in her dormitory ganged up on her in an effort to make her apostatise. Who do you think the women had as their leader? Poor Shay Yung. But they failed in their efforts to make her apostatise. Tai Yang told me afterwards she felt very weak and cried all the night long as the women tormented her.

Of course, I realised that persecution was taking place in that college where Shay Yung and Tai Yang had attended the courses. But I reasoned myself into believing that this was not the official communist policy, and that it was the work of the intellectuals who ran the courses. How blind I was!

Another incident concerned Wang Gee Poo, a native of Nancheng county and a young communist in his first fervour. He hated the Church according to Thoni, who had been in his class in Nancheng middle school. One afternoon, in April 1950, I was in the parish dispensary when I heard the sound of loud voices singing in the church. I rushed out and found Wang Gee Poo and the communist youth leader for the county standing in the centre of the church pointing to the tabernacle and laughing derisively. I noted that he and his companions carried revolvers. From a dozen to twenty blue-coated communist youth, boys and girls, were standing round the harmonium. 'This is a sacred place,' I said to Wang Gee Poo, 'and you have no right to be here, so please leave.' 'Our country is a sacred place, too,' he barked, 'and you have no right in it.' 'This church is our building and we can do what we like in it. Chairman Mao tells us there is freedom of religion and you come here to insult and mock at religion,' I said. 'You are disobeying Chairman Mao's law.' Enraged, the youth leader gave me a short lecture on my crimes and then he and Wang Gee Poo stalked out of the church followed by the singers, all jeering and hissing as they left. As soon as they were gone, I locked and barred the heavy wooden doors of the church. Later I removed the tabernacle to the house where I lived and the people came to visit the Blessed Sacrament in the house. Every afternoon for the next week or so, Wang gee Poo and a few others tried to push in the door of the church. Failing in that, they shouted insulting slogans like 'Down with the Church!' 'Down with the foreigner!'

Then one day, about a week later, at about 3.30p.m., I was in the dispensary when I heard the swift patter of feet (their shoes had paper soles) running along the cement path outside. The door was pushed open and in rushed three blue-coated Red youths, led by Wang Gee Poo, their rifles at the ready and they stood in front of me, pointing their rifles at me. Wang Gee Poo said, 'If you do not allow us to play the harmonium in the church then we will desecrate the Blessed Sacrament and dance on the crucifix.' Hatred blazed from his almond brown eyes. He foamed at the teeth. I could see the flecks of foam. Again, I invoked the magic name of Mao Tse Tung and the freedom of religion which he had given to us, which they were now violating.

At this, Wang Gee Poo scowled at me, turned around in a huff and left with his companions, cursing and spitting as he went. That evening I was very upset, not because I had been threatened with guns (I had got used to that), but because I felt frightened by the sheer hatred that emanated from Wang Gee Poo's face. I felt in my heart that there was a satanic element in Communism that day. I cannot give a reasoned explanation for this feeling but I can say in the words of Pascal that, 'the heart has its reasons which the mind knows not.'

Having felt as I did, why did I not realise that we were suffering a real persecution? Because I knew Wang Gee Poo was a careerist and I thought he was acting ultra vires to further his career. Even some of the old communist soldiers spoke disparagingly of Wang Gee Poo, as a careerist in a hurry, always trying to ingratiate himself with the Commissar. Now, thanks to the Book of Revelation and commentary, I could see clearly for the first time that the two incidents described were part of an unofficial persecution. Reading the book slowly and prayerfully provided me with an orientation course for persecution.

I shared my new thinking with the Catholics who came to the dispensary and I asked them to pass on what I told them to other fervent Catholics. I assured them that the Red guarantees for freedom of religion were mere lip service, that the persecution had already started and that soon we would be called on to make sacrifices for our faith and to give witness. Far from daunting them, the sad news I brought them seemed to call forth the best from them, and their best was excellent. They reminded me that Catholics in the village had suffered persecution after the Taiping Rebellion a hundred years earlier. Our Lady of Fatima has warned us, they said, that we must expect persecution and they were expecting it. However, Our Lady had also promised that she would help the persecuted. In this dialogue I got more from these good people than I gave them. Thus the dispensary became a resistance cell where we discussed every aspect of the communist threat. The women were

the backbone of our little resistance cell. Hopefully, what that difficult, mysterious but beautiful book taught me, I shared with the cell.

The problem of how to use the homilies on Sunday to strengthen
the people's faith and prepare them for the ordeal ahead without
provoking the Reds to stop people going to Mass or to arrest me
was a tricky one. From our discussions in the dispensary, the homilies seemed to emerge as a matter of course. Gratitude and appreci-
ation of our faith, witness to our faith, sacrifices made for their faith
by Chinese Catholics in past persecutions, Christian hope-homilies
of that type seemed to be the most helpful. There was just one
theme: that was faith under pressure, and the homilies that
emerged were just variations on that theme.

The time was not yet ripe when I could tell the people, and the Red
spies in the church on Sunday, everything I had been telling those
who came to the dispensary. If the pastor does not give bold witness in his preaching, he cannot expect his parishioners to give
'bold witness' in their practice when the testing times come. We all
knew the timing of this sermon was of essence. It seemed I would
have to wait till something happened which would lend credibility
to my assertion that the Reds were already persecuting us and were
determined to destroy the Catholic Church. But if I waited too long,
the Reds might stop the Catholics from coming to church or put me
in jail and I would thereby miss the opportunity of giving bold witness from the pulpit. Time was running out.

But there was another problem. The Wang Gee Poo factor was getting us all down. I was afraid Patrick and Thoni would break under
the intolerable strain and that they would leave me. Wang Gee
Poo's tactics varied from day-to-day but not a day went by that he
did not give us a scorching. As another priest described it, he
turned us over on the gridiron regularly. So close a watch did he
keep on our activities that we thought it better to disband the Junior Praesidia of the Legion of Mary. We feared Wang Gee Poo
might put pressure on the children and force them to tell him about
the senior Legion and its activities. It was with great regret that we
took the step. However, the Junior Praesidia members had been
trained to be little apostles, to run meetings and to report on their
work at the weekly meeting. The training should bring spiritual
dividends to the Church in the years ahead.

Wang Gee Poo's next ploy was to come to Mass on Sundays with a company of his revolver-carrying henchmen. They would stand at the back of the church as the men were coming back to their seats after receiving Holy Communion and the Reds would accost them and ask them mockingly, 'That little wafer you have received, has it filled you to repletion?' After the questions, they laughed mockingly. The people were shocked and outraged. If I confronted Wang Gee Poo because he was violating the law, he would devise something worse for the next Sunday, possibly prevent the people from coming to Mass or there would be recriminations against Thoni and Patrick. If I reported him to the Commissar that would be a commendation for him, or they might forbid me to say Mass. In this dilemma, I found myself sighing and longing for the security of a prison cell. In the cell, I would have only myself to look after, whereas in the parish there were six hundred souls to be shepherded through the fires of persecution. As Bishop Cleary had said in his apology he gave to the communists in Nancheng, I was lacking both in age and wisdom. The Holy Spirit, whom I had recently 'discovered', was lacking in neither. He would guide the people when I was out of his way. Had I not told the Catholics everything in the dispensary and would not the Reds be less repressive if I were in jail? In the cell, could I not offer my privations for my people?

All common sense, all very plausible, but a subtle temptation all the same. It took me some time to see it as a temptation which distracted me from my responsibility and lowered my morale. The pastor's place during persecution is with his people, as long as he can manage it, by hook or by crook. But I was buffeted by other temptations, the temptation to be cautious about preaching sermons that might seem provocative to the communists, like sacrifices which Catholics must be prepared to make for their faith, etc. Temptations to leave very well alone, to let sleeping mastiffs lie, to be careful not to get the people into trouble. During persecution there's no shortage of excellent reasons for not preaching painful and unpopular sermons, which the pastor is in duty bound to preach.

A very effective antidote against such temptations was passages from the Book of Ezekiel regarding the shepherds of Israel. The Book of Ezekiel belongs to the same genre of sacred literature as the Book of Revelation. The author of the Book of Revelation, it is said, was much influenced by Ezekiel. That is what attracted me to Eze-kiel. Whereas I hoped that the Book of Revelation would throw light on persecution, I hoped Ezekiel would help me to be a better pastor. Ezekiel severely castigated the shepherds and watchmen of Israel during the Babylonian captivity 2500 years ago. I felt that Ezekiel's words were for me in my unique situation in 1950. Ezekiel was no word-mincer and he warned the shepherds of Israel that if they saw the sword, the danger coming, but did not warn the flock with the trumpet, then Yahweh would hold them responsible for the fate of the flock. (Ezek 33:2-6). I do not know what effect Eze-kiel's castigations had on the shepherds of Israel but I can assure you they scared the pastor of Kiutu. They dispelled quickly my daydreams about the security of a prison cell. When it was my duty to be watchman of the flock, I must continue on painful and unpop-ular sermons. For if the 'trumpet' gave an uncertain sound who should prepare himself for battle? (1 Cor 14:8).

My temptations behind me, I have no recollection of angels coming to minister to me, but I remember very clearly that Wang Gee Poo came again to scourge Thoni and Patrick and me. This time, he accused Thoni of teaching the children Christian doctrine in the church during school hours and of forcing them to come to the school. Thoni was furious and said the charges were false and, true to form, Wang Gee Poo said he would put him in jail if he did not apostatise. At this stage, the Commissar came along and entered the discussion on the side of sweet reasonableness and told Wang Gee Poo that freedom of religion was our right. He also told him I had been very good to the poor. He then turned to Thoni and said that the children should be allowed to wait until they're old enough to decide whether they want religious instruction or not. Despite our protests that the Catholic parents had asked us to give instruction to their children, Wang Gee Poo prevented the children from coming and warned the parents, who were deeply dejected at this turn of events, right through the parish.

Then a few weeks later, a communist civilian administrator was appointed to the district. Soon the Catholics reported to me that the new administrator loathed Wang Gee Poo. Heartened by their reports, Patrick, Thoni and I paid a courtesy call on the new admin-istrator. He received us courteously and his wife came out to talk to us in a friendly manner. She had been to the dispensary and I had given her some medicine. Anyhow, we told the administrator how Wang Gee Poo had stopped the children from coming to catechism class. 'What is catechism?' the administrator asked. We told him and showed him the catechism; he looked at it and remarked. 'This is Bishop Cleary's catechism.' We told him that Bishop Cleary was, in fact, the author. Then he asked us, 'Is there anything about Communism in this catechism?' 'Nothing,' we replied in unison. We finished by telling him that Catholic children in Nancheng were allowed to attend catechism class and asked him if we could possibly start again. He said he would look into the matter and within a week had given permission to resume classes and we were overjoyed.

CHAPTER 10

The Patriotic Christian Church Movement

In July 1950, the Reds launched the Patriotic Christian Church Movement. Its aim, they said, was to purify the Christian Churches in China of all foreign elements so that all became self-governing, self-propagating, self-supporting. After they had made this announcement, there followed a bitter and sustained attack on the Pope in the communist press. He was reviled in cartoons and depicted as an Imperialist and as a tool of the Americans.

We were fortunate that we were living in South China. The Patriotic Church Movement was started in the north and we had an opportunity of seeing what the communist newspaper was saying, of reading between the lines and reaching our own conclusions. Our Catholics were very shrewd. Their conclusion was that the aim of the Patriotic Church Movement was to force Roman Catholics to reject the Pope. They knew that rejecting the Pope meant that they ceased to be Roman Catholics. At last the opportunity for which we were waiting had come.

Now that the time was ripe, I put a lot of prayer and preparation into that special sermon which I felt had to be preached. It was the most difficult sermon I have ever had to preach. When the Sunday came, our Red guest spies were in their places, as usual, well before Mass. Indeed, it seemed to me that they listened more attentively than the 'children of light'. Other Sundays their presence might have inhibited me somewhat. Not on this particular day – my words were partly for them so that they could report to the Red authorities. More importantly, my words were for the Catholics, although most of them would have heard them privately in the dispensary or from the teachers already. Most importantly, the sermon was the pastor's public and painful witness in the presence of Catholic and communist alike, and it was an effort to state the issues clearly and to dispel confusion.

The first issue I had to clarify was that the communists had been deceiving us when they had promised freedom of religion. I did this. The second issue was that the persecution had already started and that its aim was to destroy our Catholic faith that came to us from the apostles. The objective, as even the communist papers showed, was to force Catholics to reject the Pope as head of the Roman Catholic Church. North of the Yangtse, I told them, Catholics had already been asked to sign documents rejecting the Pope, the Vicar of Christ. Soon the document or a similar one would be presented to us here and we would be asked to sign it, I informed them. St Patrick's exhortation to his Irish converts 1500 years ago was, 'Ut Christiani ita et Romani sitis', 'As you are Christians, so be you also Romans,' or if you would, 'As you are of Christ, so also you must be of Rome.' Another saying from the early centuries of the Church, I reminded them, was, 'Where Peter is, there is the Church.' That saying was valid for us in our present situation. The Pope is head of the Church on earth and this has always been the faith of Catholics. We must be prepared to make every sacrifice, even life itself, rather than renounce our faith. If we in Kiutu are called to witness and to suffer, Our Lord's promise to stay with us always, even to the end of time, will sustain us. That was the gist of the sermon. "Be faithful to death, and I will give thee the crown of life," from the Book of Revelation, was our watchword.

To be quite candid, in retrospect, I think it was something of an anti-climax, because most of it was taken up with advising the people how to counteract the tactics the communists used in other places to force Catholics to join the Patriotic Church. But persecution is no time for rhetoric. After the pastor has prayed and prepared to the best of his ability he can console himself by the know-ledge that, as preacher, he is only the instrument of the Holy Spirit and that he can afford to leave a lot to the Divine Instrumentalist. Though previously I never gave him much credit for achievement, I discovered that the Holy Spirit is an over-achiever during persecution. Of course, he has a long experience in this field.

Anyhow, a great sense of relief and peace came over us that Sunday and there was an even deeper bond of unity and Christian fellowship, reminiscent of what one reads about in the Acts of the Apostles. Of course, we knew that things would not be the same again, and that we had entered a new critical phase in our relationship with the communists. Strangely enough though, there was no reaction at all from the Reds.

Everything became so ominously calm that we feared a storm might blow up at any time. Instead two priest visitors blew in and what a pleasant surprise their visits were for us. The first visitor was Luke Teng, who afterwards died after long imprisonment in a Red jail. I cannot remember how he got permission to travel as he lived in our county. What I do remember is that he preached in our church, on the Feast of the Assumption, a deeply moving sermon. Our communist guest spies didn't turn up on Holy Days of Obligation. From the back of the church, I could hear this man, who had been received into the Catholic church at the age of thirteen, tell the Catholics that they must be prepared to die rather than renounce their faith, and I marvelled at the vitality and the power in Christianity.

Still, the deep feeling and the strong conviction with which Luke Teng spoke on that Feast of the Assumption should not have surprised me because of an incident which had happened about a year earlier. I was visiting with Luke Teng, as we were good friends and visited each other as often as we could. However, during this particular visit of mine, we had a very unpleasant surprise. One morning we were talking in Luke's study when in came the Commissar unannounced. My Commissar had also jurisdiction over Pakan where Luke Teng was parish priest. The Commissar was pleasant enough until he got up to leave; then he turned to Luke Teng with anger in his eyes and said as he pointed to me, 'When we have dealt with this criminal as he deserves, and with his confreres who have brought superstition to our country, then you will become a member of the patriotic Chinese and renounce your superstition.' Luke Teng answered very gently, 'It is not superstition. It is my faith, I believe in it, and I'm prepared to die for it.' What a blessing it was, for the Catholics and especially for the converts to have this excellent Chinese priest visit us and preach to us – and indeed for the pastor. Although he had been in no way impeded in his ministry or hadn't got into any kind of trouble, still he was very pessimistic about the future. He felt we could expect nothing but suffering and persecution from the communists.

A week later, the second visitor arrived, unexpected too. He was

Mike Halford, a pal since seminary days and a fellow Columban. He was six years older than me and was Gaelic Football captain the year I entered the seminary. We played side-by-side in the forward line of our Gaelic football team. Travelling was not restricted in his county and relations between the communists and himself were excellent. A razor-sharp mind and an outrageous sense of humour, his proficiency at Chinese was such that the Reds from northern China asked him to act as interpreter between them and his parishioners when they took over the place. He spoke and understood Mandarin perfectly and spoke his local dialect like a native. I believe he also had a smattering of two other dialects. After we had exchanged experiences and news and jokes, I asked him about our future. He said 'Cheer up, they will give us the option of being shot, anyhow.' What he meant was that it was unlikely that we would be brain-washed or tortured. That possibility, though, he did not rule out, as his first practical suggestion was that we put a profession of faith on paper and give it to some of the Catholics as soon as possible. A note should be attached to the profession of faith saying that if we priests disappeared and, if afterwards, the communists attributed statements to us contrary to those in the profession of faith, then such statements were made when we were broken by brain-washing or torture, or that the statements were false. Still, at that time, he felt being shot was much more likely. 'You know,' he said, 'the custom here in China when priests are being shot is to sing the Divine Praises, the same as the Catholics sing them at Benediction. We can rehearse this evening.' After supper, he played the Divine Praises on the little harmonium we had in the house and we sang them, till we made the rafters ring. After we had rehearsed the Divine Praises a number of times – and here are the first four in romanised script:

Tsan Mi Tien Chiu
Tsan Mi Tien Chiu Shin ren
Tsan Mi Wu Chiu Yaysu Chi ti ssu te, gin Tien Chiu yi gen ren
Tsan Mi Yaysu Ti Shin min.

– we would chat away for a bit and have a smoke. Then Mike would proclaim the legend with mock humility, 'You know, there are only about a dozen songs I sing really well. Let us start with "The Harp that Once Through Tara's Halls".' Each night he was with me the ritual was repeated, Divine Praises first then songs of our land.

The second night a hitch occurred during our rehearsal. I should have said that Mike was a self-confessed tenor and that I was a self-presumed, a discredited, off-key, baritone. After we had gone through the Divine Praises he stopped playing suddenly and looked at me disapprovingly and said, 'You know you're off key there.' And then a little more sharply, 'For God's sake, Luke, don't let down the side by singing the Divine Praises out of tune when they're shooting you.' According to one man, my response to Mike's outburst of artistic temperament was, 'Mike, maybe you should lend me a tuning fork so that I can end on the right note when I am being shot.' I also remember telling him that in the words of the poet 'All discord is but harmony, not understood'.

Looking back, now, I ask myself were we play-acting during these rehearsals? I do not think so. Uppermost in Mike's mind when he abruptly suggested the rehearsals was, I believe, the case of Fr Theunisson. Who was Fr Theunisson? He was a Dutch Vincentian working in an American Vincentian Diocese bordering ours. Charlie Quinn was his bishop. Fr Theunisson's parish was about fifteen miles from Mike Halford's place and about thirty from me. He was a friend of Mike's and I never met Fr Theunisson but had heard a lot about him. He would have been about sixty-five at this particular time. One night in May 1950, at about 11.00 p.m. there was a knock on Fr Theunisson's door. Two young Reds were outside and they told him that there was an urgent call in the village and that they would take him to the sick person. He did not return. After a few hours his curate, a Chinese priest, who was awaiting him got anxious, reported the matter to the communists. Early the next morning, Fr Theunisson was found dead in a rice field about a mile outside the town and he had two bullets in his head. The communists arrested his curate on suspicion and organised a bandit hunt on the theory that the bandits might have murdered Fr Theunisson. In his last words, I am sure Fr Theunisson witnessed to the faith that brought him to China and for which in the last analysis he gave his life. If martyrdom is witness to the faith consecrated by the testimony of blood, then he was a martyr or thereabouts.

Nearly two years later, I was to hear Bishop Cleary say to a Chinese priest (whom he thought was going to be shot), 'I will give you my blessing now before you go and, when they are taking you out to shoot you, sing the Divine Praises.' My own feeling is that the pastor called on to witness with his life feels that his last words may inspire his people to persevere in their faith and that this may compensate to some degree for his inadequacies, in prayer and work, as a pastor. Mike and I often had talked about Father Michael Pro S.J., who died a martyr in Mexico in the twenties of this century. When the communists were shooting him he shouted, 'Long Live Christ the King', 'Viva el Christo Rey'. He followed the tradition they have in the Spanish-speaking world. The symbolism and the power of such words was brought home to me by an excerpt from a recent book, 'Against all Hope: The Prison Memoirs of Armando Valladares.' The author is a Cuban, an acclaimed poet, and recalls the twenty-two years of hell he spent in a Castro jail. Here is the excerpt:

> Those cries of the persecuted patriots, "Long live Christ the King!" "Down with Communism!" had wakened me to a new life. The cries became such a potent and stirring symbol that by 1963, the men condemned to death were gagged before being carried out to be shot. The jailers feared those shouts – the rebellious, defiant gesture at the supreme moment, could easily become a bad example for the soldiers. It might even make them think of what they were doing.

But rehearsing for death was a practical proposition, too, for us because life was so cheap and so unpredictable. As I have said, Mike had no trouble in his parish and so he had plenty of time to reflect on how suddenly and unexpectedly death came to Fr Theunisson and how advisable it was – for us – to be ready.

As well as that, Mike had a close friend in the communist administration in his area. He called the friend George when talking to me about him. George gave him all the information about the church north of the Yangtse and in other parts of China and about priests who had suffered like Fr Theunisson or in other ways. I needed someone with his information and experience to guide me and his visit to the Catholics and to myself was a godsend.

We had prepared and rehearsed for every eventuality and waited for the communists to make the next move. As we waited, I found the prayers of the Mass becoming much more meaningful for me. I think, in particular, of a prayer in the Canon (as it was then). It is Eucharistic Prayer No 1 now. The prayer is 'For ourselves, too, we ask some share in the fellowship of your Apostles and Martyrs, with John the Baptist, Stephen, Matthias, Barnabas, Ignatius, etc.' That fellowship became a reality to me. I realised for the first time how the Church transcends place and time. In that fellowship, I felt I was holding hands across the centuries, so to speak, with pastors who suffered persecution through the Church's history right back to that magnificent martyr and bishop, St Ignatius of Antioch. With that fellowship I felt I was in solidarity and in it I felt new-found support. Since the visits of Luke and Mike, I had a deeper sense of God's presence, of God's providence presiding over the smallest details of our lives and a consequent light-heartedness and inner peace. With hindsight, I would now describe how I felt as, 'a deepened awareness of the presence and power and workings of the Holy Spirit in our lives'.

I think the people, to some extent, shared this awareness. God's precious gift of humour never deserted us in the parish even when the outlook was anything but bright. The standard of jokes amongst priests and people in those days was of a very high quality. Yu Shin Faih was a carpenter by trade but a jokesmith by calling. Whenever he heard a new funny story or fashioned a new joke in his joke-smithy, he would come running up the steps that led to the church to share it with me and with the teachers. The stories were often unflattering to the People's Army of Liberation but invariably funny with a distinctive Chinese flavour. If, as Leon Bloy tells us, Christian joy is the surest sign of the presence of the Holy Spirit in our midst, he was very much in evidence amongst us just then.

St Thomas Aquinas teaches that though the Holy Spirit is already dwelling in the soul, there can be a new sending of the Spirit. One of his examples of occasions when this may happen is times of martyrdom.

CHAPTER 11

The Land Division

Around this time, too, the communists didn't seem to be causing us any trouble. They came to the dispensary but were usually courteous. We felt that the seeming change in attitude to us was due to the fact that the Commissar and Wang Gee Poo were away on a training course in the capital of the Province but when the Commissar did come back, he seemed to be a changed man too. We hear a lot of talk nowadays about born-again Christians, but he appeared like a born-again communist. The day of his return to Kiutu he came into the dispensary all smiles, shook hands with me and told me about the training course. The Governor of the Province, he told me, had reminded them that foreigners must be protected and that freedom of religion must be given to Catholic priests and to the Catholic Church and he had no alternative except to do as the governor ordered them to do.

There was, however, he said, one little matter about which he would like to speak to me. As the church owned land in the village, I belonged to the landlord class. Being a landlord was a capital crime but he would overlook the crime in my case. Of course, when land division came he would take most of the church land from me but he promised, with a gesture of great magnanimity, that he would leave me enough rice land to maintain myself. There was a condition attached, he added. I must till the land myself and work in the rice fields like the Chinese farmers. My reply was that I had no interest in it. If I, as a foreigner, worked in the rice fields during the tropical summer, I would die of heat-stroke. He bowed in agreement and changed the subject.

He told me about the Chinese armed forces and assured me that the Chinese would have the atomic bomb in fifteen years. He told me how much the atomic bomb would cost in rice and the figure was astronomical but I forget what exactly it was. He then asked me most graciously if I could let him have some medicine and when I gave him what he wanted, he departed all bows and smiles. A surge of hope swept through the community. Even Wang Gee Poo ceased to threaten us. The news from other parishes was that things looked better.

Then on the 8th December, the Commissar came to see me around mid-day. He looked nervous and grim. After spitting on the floor, and scratching his head a few times, he informed me that land division was starting in our district on this very day. On no account was I to leave the church for the next three months. All assemblies, except communist assemblies, were forbidden. Catholics were not to come to church services. Word got around the village that the Commissar had suspended all church services for the time being and the people were very upset. To my surprise, an unusually large crowd turned up for Benediction that evening. Many in the crowd were Catholics who, in ordinary circumstances, were lax, even about Sunday Mass and certainly never attended Benediction during my time in the parish. Yet, in periods of trouble or challenge, their old Catholic blood asserted itself and they became not only professing but aggressively practising Catholics. Many parishioners were drafted by the communists to help in the work of land division and the Bishop dispensed these from the obligation of Sunday Mass attendance.

Of course, I told the Commissar, when he informed me that there were to be no assemblies of any kind, that I could not ask the people not to come to Mass, but that I would consult my Bishop.

So the day after, I toddled into Nancheng and talked it over with the Bishop. He said that the bishops of the Province seemed to be of the opinion that we should lie low during land division and they were hopeful that after land division was over, we could co-exist with the communists. 'It is only a matter of three months,' he emphasised, 'and don't worry if some of the usual congregation don't come to Mass. A number of them are dispensed anyhow.' As I walked the ten miles home to Kiutu I realised that the bishops of the Province had an overview of the situation which I did not possess and that they had good reason for being hopeful. Nevertheless, from my own experience in my little parish, I could not share their hope.

The next Sunday at Mass, we had a smaller attendance than usual and at daily Mass we had mostly older people. For some days it looked as if land division was not going to affect the Church adversely after all, till one night around 4.00 a.m. I heard a loud persistent knocking on the door. It was an old Catholic man and he was crying bitterly. He told me the Commissar, at a meeting of the Peasants' Association the previous night, had read out a list of my crimes. At the end of the list was a resolution demanding that I be punished severely. When the members of the Association refused to sign their names to the resolution, the Commissar behaved like a raving lunatic. 'He and his minions begin to beat us,' continued my visitor, 'and when that failed, he took out a gun and pointed it at us in a threatening manner. A number of us signed. I am deeply sorry I signed,' he said as he wept. 'You have helped me when I was hungry', he continued, 'but if I didn't sign it would be the end of me. Now that I have signed, I know that it is the end of you. I could not sleep with remorse so I decided to get up and tell the Sen Fu. Let the Commissar find out if he will.'

I tried to console Ngo Ssu (which was the visitor's nickname), and I thanked him for the invaluable information he had brought me at great risk to himself. Ngo Ssu means 'Dead with the Hunger'. He liked the name and had a great sense of humour. He had only enough rice of his own to tide him over three months out of twelve. The parish managed to supply him with rice for the remaining nine months.

During land division, a special squad of spies patrolled the village and the area, and the Catholics feared them so much that few of them came to the dispensary. The day before Christmas Eve, the village was electric with tension. A couple of landlords had been shot after suffering torture, three committed suicide, sons had been brain-washed into 'ganging up' against parents and accusing the parents of being landlords. Such was the atmosphere of tyranny and terror in the parish as the season of peace and good will approached.

I knew my people. I knew they would want to celebrate the Christmas feast come what may; and at 4.30 p.m. on Christmas Eve, Yu Shin Faih, the carpenter, came. 'Sen Fu, the communists will start supper at 5 p.m., they will be drinking wine tonight and they won't be finished till 6.30 p.m. or so. The older Catholics, forty or fifty of them, will take the risk of coming to Mass in the church. Can you be there to hear their confessions?' When I said I would be delighted, he suggested that the rest of the Catholics would come during the night.

A sizeable crowd of older members of the congregation was there at 5 p.m. During the persecution the Nuncio, Archbishop Riberi, had given us faculties to say Mass wearing just a stole and starting at the Eucharistic Prayer. So the Mass was short and I was able to spend over an hour hearing confessions. The congregation had gone before the Reds had finished supper. Well-pleased with the enterprise and daring of the community, I let some of them know, as they left the church, that I would say two Masses during the night if they could pick a suitable time.

Around 2 o'clock in the morning I heard a knock and Thoni, one of the teachers, whispered, 'The Catholics have come.' I rushed to the church. The night was frosty and bitterly cold. We did not dare to light even a candle because the local militia might see it and drive away the people. We would most certainly be charged with unlawful assembly by night and God only knows what the penalty would be. We had to be content with the dim gleam of the sanctuary lamp but it was sufficient to enable me to distribute Holy Communion and I did not need to do any reading as I knew the Eucharistic Prayer by heart. For a couple of hours I heard Confessions and then said my second Mass. More Confessions followed and then my third Mass. The faith and the fervour of the Catholics that Christmas night is one of my most cherished memories. Somehow persecution brings out all that is best in each of us.

After Communion at the third Mass, I could hear the women in the dark church sobbing softly, but bitterly. These poor people hungered for the Bread of Life and they knew that a soul famine would soon come over the land. They realised that they would suffer spiritual starvation when the Breadwinner would be taken away from them. They sensed they were attending their last Christmas Mass for a long time to come. Still sobbing, they left the church and wended their way down the steps that lead to the village.

The next day I was in the dispensary when, at about half past eleven, two men of the local communist organisation came to me. They were now officers in the local militia. One of them was Di Yi Hou whose wife was a Catholic. I knew him well as I had dressed his ulcerated leg many times in the dispensary. They produced a summons from the Commissar bidding me to appear at once before the People's Court in the Assembly Hall in our orphanage.

When I entered the Assembly hall, I was surprised to see all the villagers gathered there round the Commissar, who stood in the centre. I could see Lorenzo's furniture on display near the opposite wall. Lorenzo was a native of the parish, but had been comprador (buyer) in the church in Nancheng for some years. After the Reds came, he asked me to store some furniture for him. I notified the Reds and they gave permission, but not in writing. Since land division Lorenzo, though by no means a rich man, had been declared a landlord. Here I was before the People's Court charged with sabotaging the Land Reform Movement by harbouring a landlord's property.

The Commissar called for silence and, pointing his left hand dramatically in the direction of the furniture, with the index finger of his right hand pointed at me, he roared, 'See, how this foreigner violates the people's laws. He hides the landlord's property, thereby depriving the poor of their rights. He's an oppressor of the poor.' After a pause he reminded the people that this was the People's Court and that they had the right and duty to punish me as I deserved. The people seemed bored.

By this time, he had worked himself into a frenzy, fixing his eyes on me with a half-demented stare. He screamed at the people and urged them to be patriotic and punish those who violated their laws. The people did not seem unduly excited by the violation of their laws and they just listened impassively. When he finished his tirade, I told the Court gently that we had permission to store Lorenzo's furniture as everybody knew. 'You have no written proof,' roared the Commissar. 'You have no proof,' chanted too the two men who had summoned me to the court. 'You have no proof,' said a voice from the hall and I looked back to see whose the voice was. I was flabbergasted when I discovered that it was the voice of Niao, the teacher who had asked for the instruction in the Catholic faith a few months earlier. He had begged that I, and not one of the teachers, give him instruction. Now my eyes were opened and I realised that he was a spy 'planted' on us by the Reds. I was very annoyed at my lack of discernment seeing that I had always spoken so glibly about discernment in conversation with the Bishop and the priests in Nancheng, but I was amazed that the people or the teachers did not recognise he was a spy from the beginning – the Chinese are so shrewd. After they had photographed me with Lorenzo's furniture and Lorenzo's sister-in-law, the Commissar said to the soldiers, 'Take him away.' Of course, I objected to the pictures being taken but the Commissar sent a number of soldiers to force me and I didn't think it was worth making an issue of the incident. To my surprise, they led me back to the church. They kept me under heavy guard for the rest of the day. I was depressed because, above all, this looked like the end. Patrick, however, consoled me. 'Don't worry,' he said, 'it will be only six months in jail and you'll be back.' Next morning, I said Mass very early. The people at Mass were in tears as they left the Church.

An hour later, I was arrested and brought before the commissar and his staff. The charges were that I had not only sabotaged the Revolution, but also the Patriotic Church and Land Reform. The Commissar lectured me for my crimes and deplored them and said, 'I lack the jurisdiction to deal with a criminal of your calibre. You are being sent under guard to Nancheng to-day.' 'May another priest come here to take my place,' I asked. 'No, no,' he replied emphatically, 'the Church here has been overthrown.'

I was allowed to take a change of clothing and as much of my possessions as would fit into two small baskets. An armed soldier and a member of the local militia constituted my escort. Patrick and Thoni, faithful to the end, came too, but the people were forbidden to assemble to see me off. One old man, Wang Dee Ni, Wang Bay Hua's father, awaited me at the bottom of the steps, the tears rolling down his cheeks. He shouted, 'If and when you go back to your country, will you ask the people to pray for us. Your people have been through persecution in the past and they can understand what we are suffering now.' 'I certainly will,' I assured him. Whenever I think of my expulsion from the parish, a line of French poetry comes to mind; it is 'Partir, c'est mourir un peu' (To part is to die a little). Perhaps we die in stages.

Something in me died that day. There is no other pastoral experience quite like going through persecution with one's people. The experience forges a bond between people and priest that time cannot sever, I discover – thirty years later.

As I turned for Nancheng, I gave a last look at the village on the hill which in peacetime was a veritable Arcadia and even in its darkest days left me with memories that were bitter-sweet.

My guards were quite courteous till we reached the city. Then they hustled me a bit – perhaps they were showing off – till we reached the county Commissar's office. The Commissar was a stout grey-haired man with broad stooped shoulders. He showed little interest in our arrival. He read the document given him by my guards and put his seal on the note which he gave to a blue-coated attendant who was standing by. We were sure that our next stop would be jail and Patrick whispered to me, 'Explain to the Commissar now before it's too late.' So I said, 'Excuse me, County Commissar, could I explain?' He replied calmly that I could explain at my trial. To our surprise, the blue-coated boy didn't take us to the jail, but said in a peremptory manner, 'To the church.'

The note which the blue-coated boy brought along was for Bishop Cleary. It said I was not to be put in the ordinary civilian jail just yet, but that, as a prisoner of the People's Government, I was to be placed in captivity in the church compound with the Bishop as my jailer until my trial, which was scheduled for the next day. Strange to relate, I wasn't that happy going to the church because when I was the first priest of the diocese declared a criminal by the communists, I had got the Bishop and the priests in Nancheng into trouble, and here I was at it again! Every other priest in the Diocese seemed to be unaffected, in a serious manner anyhow, by the new regime. It looked as if I was finished as pastor, but persecution seemed to be only beginning.

CHAPTER 12

Criminals Galore

We were warmly welcomed by Jim Yang and Tom Fisher when we reached the church compound, complete with our escort. Tom took the note from the blue-coat and brought it up to the Bishop. The Bishop had to sign a statement to the effect that I would always be on hand whenever the Reds would summon me and that I would not leave the church compound. The Bishop signed as requested and the blue-coat took back the note. Before leaving, however, he gave us to understand that my trial would take place next day and he ordered Patrick and Thoni to stay in town. The Bishop was very sympathetic and welcoming and he and I went over to the Columban Sisters' Convent for afternoon tea. It was great meeting the Sisters again and we had a very pleasant hour with them.

On our way back, the Bishop said that we should have a rehearsal for my trial in the recreation room after supper that evening. Jim Yang, who was a Chinese lawyer, would be the prosecutor and we should have Patrick and Thoni with us. Before we started the rehearsal, the Bishop warned me not to make any wisecracks during my trial the next day, and that I wasn't to make speeches from the dock either. Jim Yang warned me not to show any displeasure or irritation, no matter what the outcome of the trial was. Another thing, he warned me against, was to be careful not to make the judges, or whoever, lose face. So they asked me all the possible questions on each of the charges which the communists had levelled against me. When my response was inadequate they told me what I should say. They asked Patrick and Thoni for their opinions from time to time.

The rehearsal was very helpful and by the time it was finished, I felt fairly confident. Jim Yang then took Patrick and Thoni to his room for a chat, and the Bishop invited me to his room. After we had talked for a while, the Bishop told me that he was worried about his files on Tim Leonard, who was hacked to death by the communists in Nanfeng, and on Cornie Tierney who died in their hands. He thought that we should plan for every contingency. His general feeling was that we should get rid of any letter or document which might get the Chinese priests into trouble if ever our files fell into the communists' hands. With that end in view, we went through the files for a couple of hours and shredded some of them.

At half past six the next morning, the Bishop knocked at my door and said, 'Luke, get up for your trial; you can say Mass in my oratory upstairs as you are not allowed to leave the house and it is better not to go into the outside church'. He served my Mass and after breakfast, Thoni, Patrick and I waited for our summons to the court, but no summons came. The next day we waited again. Still no summons, but the tension was growing all the time.

Then on New Year's morning, I said Mass at about 7 o'clock and then I went down to the side door of the Bishop's house and a most unexpected sight greeted my eyes. It was Mick Moran wearing a black soutane and American army boots with a halter slung around his neck being escorted by six young soldiers to the Bishop's house. He seemed to be on the verge of collapse, so I rushed down and helped him up the steps. His face was pale, sickly green. I helped him into Tom Fisher's room.

He soon revived and realised for the first time that I was in Nancheng on a New Year's morning, when I should be in my parish. 'What are you doing here?' he asked. 'Didn't you know that I was expelled from Kiutu four days ago?' I replied. 'What were you expelled for?' he queried. 'I have been specialising in sabotage' I replied. 'They have accused me of sabotaging the Revolution, the Land Reform and the Patriotic Church Movement.' 'So you're a criminal, too,' he cried with ill-concealed joy. Mick Moran had been over twenty years in China and had never taken a holiday. He had become more orientalised than any other Columban missionary and he felt the 'loss of face' implied in his expulsion much more than any of us young missionaries would have felt it. Therefore, he was delighted to find that he was not the only criminal.

Then one of his armed bodyguards asked me to get the Bishop. It turned out that both the bishop and Jim Yang had to go to the Mandarin's office to bail out Mick Moran. He was given over to the

Bishop's care and the Bishop was to see that he, like myself, was on hand any time the Reds summoned him.

Mick was so ill that the hospital doctor sent him to bed immediately and told him he must stay there for several weeks. His blood pressure was astronomically high; so high that he should have been dead. Tom Fisher, strange to say, got a very severe back pain the night before Mick arrived and was confined to bed. So between visiting Mick in one room and Tom Fisher in the other, I was pre-occupied and forgot my crimes and impending trial.

About three days after Mick's arrival he had improved a lot and one evening, when the Bishop and Barney O'Neill were visiting him, he was able to give us an outline of his story.

Mick had got on very well with the Red Administration in his District of Song Thong Shui. In fact, he had invited them out shooting on a few occasions. As Mick had been twenty years in China, it was only to be expected that some of the local people would make charges against him when the Reds came. This happened a year before he was arrested, but although the communists told him about it, they did not do anything. Then on 30th December, at about 11 a.m., a blue-coated Red agent asked Mick for his shotgun. He was surprised at the request. He gave the gun to the blue-coat who had demanded it and then, about noon, Mick himself was arrested by two policemen and locked in one of the rooms of his own orphanage. The police told him that the reason for his arrest was that the people had again brought up the same charges which had been levelled against him a year earlier and that his trial would take place the following day. Somehow, he managed to scribble a note to Seamus O'Reilly and to forward it to him, telling him that he had been arrested and would be tried on the next day.

Towards nightfall, he was brought to the house and the guards stayed with him. They were chatty and sociable enough as they were local boys and Mick had often treated them in the dispensary. Mick's teacher, whose name was Chin, very cleverly said to the guards, 'It is the custom for the Sen fu to visit the church about this time every night. Could you not allow him to carry out this duty? You can accompany him yourself. It would be only for a short time'. They considered the matter for a while and eventually con-sented. In the meantime, Chin had gone out, procured the key of the tabernacle and when Mick entered the church handed it to him in an unobtrusive way. Mick then went to the tabernacle and consumed the Blessed Sacrament and returned to his house, where he was kept under guard all that night.

The next morning he was led out to his trial which took place in the church. The church had been decorated for the occasion – pictures of Chairman Mao and other Red celebrities, as well as Red flags, adorned the sanctuary. As he was led down the church the people, headed by the Farmers Association and careerists, began to boo and jeer and strike at him and call loudly for his head. One of his teachers, a Mr Dong, who apostatised during the Teachers' Training Course the previous summer, directed the accusations (Mr Dhong's brother was one of my teachers and was most faithful and loyal to the end – and since). He was accused of nearly every crime under the sun from tort to mayhem and he had many accusers. After the booing and jeering and accusing had continued for a couple of hours, the Commissar took the stage. He said he was really astonished at the number and variety of Mick's crimes. He went on to say that the people had asked for his death, but since he was a foreigner, the Commissar did not have power to execute him so he would send him to a higher authority – Nancheng.

Then a halter was thrown loosely over Mick's head and he was led down the principal streets of the town to provide a Roman holiday for the people. The people were urged to enjoy the spectacle and cheer and jeer as much as they wished, but they were not allowed to beat him. When he had paraded the town, six soldiers were detailed to escort him to Nancheng and as it was a very hot afternoon Mick felt nauseated. When they were a mile out of town the local Commissar sent a message after him telling him not to worry as his fate was nothing worse than being sent to Nancheng. The messenger then shook hands with him and departed.

When the procession had gone about five miles, Mick got ill. He was not quite sure if it was sunstroke or stomach trouble brought on by nervous tension, but he was so sick that he had to lie down on the road and rest. On account of his sickness the party was behind schedule and decided they would not be able to reach Nancheng that night so they told Mick that he could stay in a 'Fan Tien', a roadside inn, that night. In the inn, the soldiers did not go to sleep. He could hear them talking from the other side of the thin bamboo partition and one of them said, 'If he escapes we will most certainly be shot. It's well for us he got sick'. This soldier was referring to the fact that Mick was a very powerful man, about 220 lbs in weight and nearly six feet tall. He managed to sleep for a short time in the 'Fan Tien' and was wakened before dawn and the journey was completed uneventfully.

Then he told us how his teacher, Chin, had been tortured for several hours and asked to divulge where Mick had hidden his gold and other goods. Chin's wife was also tortured as was her sister who looked after the orphanage.

Then Mick said to Barney O'Neill, 'Barney, tell us about your ordeal. I have not heard your story at all.' Here is the gist of the story as Barney told it. The comprador of the church in Nancheng was declared a landlord well before Christmas. He had been arrested on Christmas Day but the communists promised they would release him and let him go back to the church if the church would guarantee that he would be available whenever the local Commissar needed him. Lorenzo, his son, whose furniture I stored in Kiutu, was delighted when he heard the news and approached Jim Yang. Jim Yang and Lorenzo went to the Bishop but the latter was chary of taking any responsibility in the matter. However, when they pointed out to him that the only responsibility entailed was that Lorenzo's father should stay in the church, he consented. Accordingly, Barney O'Neill, as Administrator, wrote a note saying that the Bishop guaranteed the man would be available and would not leave the church. The old man, the comprador, was immediately released and he was very thankful to the Bishop.

After his release, he appeared quite calm and full of Christian resignation. That night he talked until twelve o'clock with the sacristan and his wife and appeared to be in good spirits, considering what he had gone through in the days previous. At twelve o'clock he went to bed in his room which was right opposite the window of Tom Fisher's office. The next morning his room was empty and there was no sign of him any place. Finally, they dragged the pond behind the church and there they discovered his body.

The Bishop and Barney O'Neill were stunned by the news; the authorities, who were informed immediately, were enraged and accused Barney of being an accomplice of the comprador. About ten o'clock, a furious mob, led by the careerists and the local leader of the Farmers' Association entered the house. They clamoured for Barney O'Neill and accused him of sabotaging the Land Reform.

He denied the charge and explained what had happened. However, they tied his hands behind his back, put a rope around his body and led him out. When they got outside the church compound, the leader shouted to the people, 'Come along and join us; see the foreigner getting punished'. This made the mob more furious and in a short time the whole town seemed to have joined in the procession. Barney thought he was going to be murdered and he continued to make Acts of Contrition as he was being led through the street. When the procession reached the People's Court, the people got into the courtyard. He noticed a Catholic brandishing a spear, standing on duty at the gate. The officials and the mob stood in a circle round him while his crimes were read out. The mob screamed for his death. He thought he was being led to his execution when he was brought out through another passage at the end of the courtyard. At the end of the passage was a room, a pig-sty, and here he was incarcerated. Still he did not know what was going to happen and he was left in suspense for three hours. Then to his surprise, the cords were removed from his wrists and he was taken back to the church.

The explanation of his unexpected release is rather interesting. Shortly after he was arrested, a messenger was sent from the church to the county Commissar to inform him what had happened. The latter appeared annoyed and said that the local Farmers Association had no right to act contrary to the law as they had done in this case. He then telephoned The Farmers Association office and told them to release Barney. They agreed to do so but there was one snag. They demanded over a hundred American dollars from the church – the amount that the dead man owed them. The church, they claimed, had collaborated with Lorenzo's father in an act which deprived the poor people of quite a lot of money. The church, therefore, must bear the responsibility and pay up and when the compensation was paid, Barney would be released. The Bishop, fearing for Barney's safety, thought it was better to pay the compensation and Barney was set free.

When Barney had finished his story, I asked him, 'Do you really think that Lorenzo's father committed suicide or is it possible that the Reds spirited him out of his room and had him drowned?' 'Yes,' said Barney, thoughtfully, 'I've been thinking of that myself and I believe that it's quite probable. First of all, Lorenzo's father, in his conversation with the sacristan the night before, seemed quite peaceful. Besides, his shoes were not left on the steps which led down to the pond. You know how the Chinese have a custom that when a member of the family commits suicide by drowning, that member leaves his or her shoes by the side of the pond so that the relatives will know where to find the body. The old man would have followed that custom had he committed suicide and there were no shoes to be found, as I have said. Besides', he continued, 'by drowning Lorenzo's father they knew they could demand compensation from the church. They also knew they could again demand compensation from Lorenzo who was his father's heir. And you mark my words, they will demand it from him in due time even though they pretend now that they have no such intentions.'

We tried to figure out what lessons there were to be learned from Mick's story and from Barney's, but by January 8th we began to wonder if such an exercise would be very helpful.

The reasons why we began to have reservations were that on January 8th, about eight o'clock in the evening, and a very frosty and cold evening it was, we heard that Luke Teng had been arrested in his parish in Pakan, taken into Nancheng city and put into the civilian jail. The details of his arrest, as far as I could gather, were as follows. It was Luke Teng's misfortune that the Kiutu Commissar also held jurisdiction over Pakan. When the Land Reform started in Pakan, some of the Red officials from Nancheng, who had come to help in the Land Division, quartered themselves in Luke Teng's house. They made his life miserable.

In particular, there was one official from the Nancheng Police who was very insulting and on January 8th, this police official placed Luke Teng under arrest and told him he was sending him to jail in Nancheng. Luke Teng asked to be given permission to visit the church before he was taken to Nancheng. Permission was granted but the police official accompanied him. Luke Teng entered the sanctuary, opened the door of the tabernacle and proceeded to consume the Blessed Sacrament. Unfortunately, the official and his agents pinned Luke Teng's hands behind his back before he had consumed all the Hosts. I believe there were one or two sacred Hosts that he had not consumed. Luke Teng begged them to let him have the sacred Hosts but his request was refused. The official then walked through the streets of Pakan holding the sacred Hosts aloft and asking the people, the non-believers, to join him in a mock procession of the Blessed Sacrament.

The witness given by Luke Teng was outstanding. Wang Gee Poo had approached him three months earlier and had cautioned him, not to apostatise but to take part in the Patriotic Church Movement. He reminded Luke Teng how much China had suffered from Imperialism and he pointed out how the church was just a tool of the Imperialists. 'When we have driven out all these foreigners and punished them, then you will be wise and see the light,' he told Luke Teng ominously. 'Whatever happens', said Luke Teng, 'I will always believe in the Church's teaching as I now believe in it. For my convictions I'm prepared to give my life'. Wang Gee Poo left disappointed and disgusted.

Nearly a week later, on the 14th of January, on a piercing cold afternoon, I was sitting in Tom Fisher's office when the door opened and who came in unexpectedly but Fr Vincent McNally accompanied by two soldiers. He bad been expelled from his parish, Hsiao Shih, twelve miles southwest of Nancheng, that very morning. He looked thin and pinched and miserable with the cold and seemed to be much taller than he actually was. The Bishop had to sign the usual document to bail him out. After he had his supper and changed into warm clothes, he gave us the story of his crimes.

When the Land Division gathered momentum in his area, he had been charged with several crimes and his crimes covered four pages of a small copybook. The original aspect of Vincent's crimes was that many of them were committed years before he came to China. His trial took place in the church and he had to stand at the corner of the altar steps while the local Farmers Association leader read out his crimes. After ten minutes of accusations, two savage-looking thugs from the back of the church shouted in the local patois 'Yao sai geh', 'slaughter him'. Then the leader would read out some more of his crimes, then a brief silence and then the thugs would again chant their lines 'Yao sai geh'. After this had been repeated a few times, the Commissar stood up and called for reasonableness in the matter. He remarked that the people demanded that Fr McNally be punished by death but that he would send him into Nancheng to be sentenced as soon as the People's Court agreed.

He had warned the soldiers who were escorting Vincent to Nancheng to make sure that he did not commit suicide on the journey. The soldiers asked him if he had any medicine and when he replied that he had some tablets, they asked him to hand them over to them. They feared that the tablets might contain poison and that Vincent could achieve self-destruction by just swallowing a few tablets. They also took away his pocket-knife lest he might slit his throat and thereby escape the penalties of his numerous crimes. Again, they briefed his escorts. The Commissar told them to keep close watch on him whenever he got near a pond in case he might jump in. He particularly warned them to hold Vincent while he was crossing the Wan Nien Chow, as the river spanned by the bridge was the most likely place for a criminal, unable to face life, to 'shuffle off this mortal coil'. Before they reached the bridge in question, the escorts relieved him of his watch and also of his wallet which contained some money. They caught hold of his arm and linked him as they crossed the bridge fearing that he might take the fatal plunge. But even if he did plunge, my recollection is that there was only about a few inches of water in the river at that time of the year and a man of his height would have some slight difficulty in drowning himself in such shallow water.

Eventually he reached Nancheng. The magistrate, after scanning the book of his crimes, said, 'Of course, you are not answerable for all these; only for the ones which you committed yourself will you be punished.' Although Vincent was naturally very distressed at having been taken away by force from his very devoted Catholics, nevertheless he did admit to us that evening that his career as a criminal was rich in comedy and farce.

About the 30th of January, another country priest joined the Nancheng fraternity of criminals. It was none other than Mike Halford and he was accompanied by his trusty carrier whom he called 'Galloping Hogan'. When he was leaving me after his last visit to Kiutu he had offered me a bet of a dollar that he would be in jail before me and he made this gesture to boost my morale. Ladbroke's or any reputable bookies would have given 100-1 against Mike being in jail before me, because he was very friendly with the communist establishment in Kaopi and I was in trouble with my boss all the time. Anyhow, I put on the bet with him although I should have known that you couldn't win when placing a wager with Mike and the first thing he said to me when I met him in Nancheng was, 'Comrade Tien, pay the dollar you owe me.' I paid it and then he went on to tell his story to the Bishop and all the priests who had gathered in Tom Fisher's office.

On Christmas Eve, as he was preparing to hear the confessions of the country people who had come in for the feast, he was arrested. The charges were that he had a rifle and some gold bars. His gardener, 'Old Circus', had reported that Mike had paid him in gold a year previously, but Mike denied this when charged by the communist officials. He explained as best he could the complicated story of his rifle. They took him from the church and brought him to George's office where he discovered that George had a 'new look'. It was a 'red' look. Gone was the old camaraderie and bonhomie and George actually threatened Mike and shouted at him, warning that unless he showed more candour with regard to his rifle and his gold the people would have to punish him. Mike spent a sleepless night in George's office. At dawn the next morning, he was marched to Luki. The twenty mile walk, and quite a bit of it uphill, fatigued him a good deal and by the time he reached the Mandarin's office in Luki, he was well-nigh exhausted.

The Mandarin's deputy interrogated him and said sarcastically, 'I suppose there's no use asking what happened to the rifle? You probably had a watertight statement prepared ages ago.' After the interrogation, the Reds sent for Pat Sheehy, pastor of Luki, and allowed Mike to return to Luki church with the latter. He spent a few days at the church and while he was there, the Red agents came to question him. They allowed him to return to Kaopi and gave him a room. A week later they drove him from that room and told him to live in the gatehouse. He was no sooner settled there when another summons came from Luki and again he was brought back twenty miles under escort to the Mandarin's office. Again, the same questions were asked and the same threats made and again he was allowed to stay in Pat Sheehy's house. About the second or third day he was told he could return to Kaopi without an escort. This journey was the most trying part of his ordeal because he knew that some of the wild men of the People's Army of Liberation were in the area and the danger that he might suffer the same fate as that of Fr Theunisson was a real one. However, he reached Kaopi and again took up residence in the gatehouse. He was pretty miserable and finally they told him to go to Nancheng. On his way to Nancheng he was held up by the People's Militia every half hour. The landlords could be seen hanging from trees by their wrists (this was the kind of torture that was meted out to them) as he passed along. Even the children were playing games of 'Overthrowing the landlords' and 'Overthrowing the Imperialists'. As he finished his story, Mike looked at me and said, 'As I passed Kiutu I gave a long last look back and remembered the happy days we had there.'

Having digested our stories to the best of his ability, the Bishop was still hopeful. He thought that the expulsion of us four missionaries was in great part due to the Land Division upheaval. He felt, too, that some of the communists in the country areas were getting out of hand and not implicitly obeying their own superiors. Plausibility was added to his opinion by a statement made by a high communist official in Nancheng. The official in question met Jim Yang one day and assured him that in no way should we consider closing down the Catholic school in Nancheng. 'Of course,' the official said half apologetically, 'we cannot help what some of the wild men in the country do,' or words to that effect. We understood this to mean that the higher officials in Nancheng did not altogether approve of the treatment that had been meted out to us country priests. The Bishop hoped that Vincent McNally and I would be able to return to our churches as soon as Land Division was finished, say, about Easter. He did, however, realise that Mick Moran, owing to the fact that he had been so long in China and had many enemies, would not be able to return to his parish. But whatever about the protestations of the communist official who talked to Jim Yang, the wild men in the country seemed to be calling the shots.

CHAPTER 13

Violence and Visas

Day after day there were rumours of landlords and ex-officals from the Nationalist Party being shot. In the papers one read of places in the province where they had so many to shoot on a particular day that they just loaded the condemned people into a truck, drove the truck slowly along the streets and the condemned men were sprayed with machine-gun fire. One also read of sons who denounced their fathers as landlords and asked the government to punish them with death. Day after day, the orgy of hatred and violence seemed to gather momentum.

The first day of the Chinese New Year somebody rushed in to tell us that there were cartoons vilifying the church on all the billboards in the city. The cartoons were fairly big and twelve of them depicted Mick Moran feverishly perpetrating his many and various crimes. In one cartoon, he wore Rosary beads over his soutane while he was engaged in these misdemeanours. I only got six cartoons and I was shown in various aspects of my role as 'Grand Saboteur'. One of the cartoons, in particular, made Thoni and Tommy Yuy, my very loyal teacher and my friend, roar with laughter. I was shown sweeping up my house prior to welcoming a crowd of savage-looking thugs carrying Tommy-guns. They were the bandits I was supposed to have harboured. Vincent McNally got three cartoons. We were amused when we heard of the cartoons but Jim Yang and the other Chinese priests and teachers were very distressed. It seemed to them part of a campaign to smear and overthrow the Church. All the thousands of people who visited Nancheng during the New Year Festival would stop and look and study these cartoons. They seemed to have 'top billing'.

After the Chinese New Year, the Bishop decided that there was little chance of any of us being allowed to return to our parishes. He, therefore, applied for visas for Mick Moran, Mike Halford and the

Sisters. It was a good idea to try to get Mick out of the country as he was our 'ranking' criminal. It might be easier for the rest of us after his departure. Jim Yang then asked the county Commissar if Vincent McNally and I could return to our parishes around Easter. The latter did not give a direct reply, however. He did hint, though, that in some places foreign priests were treated with much more cruelty than in Nancheng. He said that he should have put Mick Moran and me in jail, but we looked so ill when we were taken in that he was afraid we would die in the local jail and that he would lose face. Mick Moran was refused a visa, but Mike Halford and the Sisters obtained theirs. They were told that they would be allowed to start their journey towards Hong Kong in a month.

But although Mick Moran didn't get a visa, he did get another public trial in Nancheng. About twenty people from his parish, some of them Catholics, in fact, were brought in to accuse him. The majority of them, though, were forced to come. The trial was held in the compound where the Commissar lived and it lasted for a few hours. Mike Halford accompanied Mick Moran and the latter was allowed to speak in his own defence this time. In fact, according to Mike Halford, it was the nearest approach to a democratic court ever held by the Reds in our area. Mick Moran's teacher, who had renounced his faith, was chief accuser and Mick put up a spirited defence and rebutted nearly all of his charges. No verdict was given and after four hours, both priests returned to the church, but the suspense weighed heavily on Mick Moran.

Most nights we four criminals played bridge and we enjoyed it immensely. Sometimes the Bishop would come down to watch the game and to hear the crack. Sometimes Tom Fisher would take a hand but he was usually busy in his office and Barney O'Neill was busy in the parish which was still running.

In that kind of relaxed atmosphere, we gradually unwound, although there was still a lot of suspense and tension. I cannot remember anything about Easter in Nancheng that year and I have nothing in my notes about it. Of course, the feast was celebrated as Nancheng parish was still functioning and if Land Division was finished in Kiutu and Hsiao Shih I'm sure there would be quite a few Catholics from both places in Nancheng for Easter Sunday.

On Easter Sunday night, however, about eight o'clock, we four criminals were playing Bridge in a downstairs room in the Mission headquarters when the door opened and a tall man strode into the room. It was Joe Flynn, assistant priest of Nanfeng Mission. We were very surprised to see him. 'What do you mean by interrupting our bridge game?' growled Mike, shaking Joe warmly by the hand. Joe sat down and told us his story. He said that the communists had taken over Nanfeng compound and that they had also taken over the parish of Lienchu. Pat Dermody of Nanfeng and Hugh Bennett, the pastor of Lienchu, were at the bus station in town and would have to spend the night there, but the guards had been lenient with him, probably because of his 'honest face' and had given him permission to spend the night in the church. He further surprised us by telling us that the three of them would have to continue their journey to Hong Kong the following morning. In fact, we had lost two parishes in this one haul, Nanfeng and Lienchu. Nanfeng was the pivot of the Southern Line, with a compound rated the most beautiful and serviceable in the whole diocese, and a walled city that exceeded Nancheng in population and wealth. Lienchu was a large country parish, fifteen miles east of Nanfeng and was an old Christianity. Hugh Bennett had been forced out of Lienchu two months earlier when his mission station was turned into the communist headquarters and he was told to take up residence in the Nanfeng mission pending further decisions in his regard. What he was not told was that in Nanfeng the local Commissar had already set his greedy eyes on the church compound and had taken over the priests' house as headquarters for himself and his staff, and converted the other buildings into a jail, one small room of which was allocated to the resident priests.

Joe told us about how, appropriately enough on Ash Wednesday, the three of them were evicted from their house and interned in this small room where all they had was plenty of fresh air, since its window was without glass. They were told to make arrangements to leave Nanfeng at once and they could either go to the headquarters in Nancheng or leave the country. They wrote to the Bishop and he, in his reply, told them there was no point in coming to Nancheng as the house was already overcrowded by other priests expelled from their parishes, and he advised them to apply for exit visas from Nanfeng. They applied but visas were held up because some months earlier Pat Dermody had sold an old motor cycle to a dealer and the Commissar claimed that the cycle had belonged to the Church and therefore now belonged to the State. Pat insisted that the motorcycle was, in fact, private property and that he was within his legal rights in selling it. The Commissar, however, demanded restitution and after much brow-beating, Pat finally agreed to pay the so-called restitution. After this problem had been cleared up, the exit visas arrived without further delay.

We felt great sympathy for the two men who would have to spend a very uncomfortable night in the bus station, but, because a curfew was in force, there was nothing we could do to provide them with some comfort. But we might have known that in China it is always the unexpected that happens! Suddenly there was a loud banging at the outside door, which alarmed us since we knew from experience that late night visitors always brought ill tidings. However, on opening the door we were delighted to find that our callers were none other than Pat and Hugh. They both looked tired and worn. Pat Dermody, the Vicar General, had spent about thirty years in China and Hugh Bennett about fifteen.

After our three guests had a meal, we had a session together and compared notes. We priests from Nancheng county were anxious to hear about how things had gone for the Church in Nanfeng county and in the southern part of the diocese. As far as I remember, Catholics in Nanfeng area had not up to them been intimidated or pressurised much. All the pressure had been put on the priests. Hugh Bennett told us that when he had been expelled from Lienchu he reported to the communist boss on his arrival in Nanfeng. The boss, who was from the north of China, (near Mongolia where the people had bread for their staple food), said to Hugh, 'Do you eat bread?' 'No', replied Hugh, 'I came walking.' In Chinese the phrases 'Do you eat bread?' and 'Did you come on horseback?' are very similar in sound. It only goes to show the pitfalls into which the feet of the unwary who try to speak Chinese can fall.

The following morning, police and customs officials came to examine the bags of our guests. The priests were forbidden to take cameras, photographs or documents of any kind with them. Then about 10.30 we said good-bye and they boarded a truck for the provincial capital Nancheng. A few days later the entire community of Columban Sisters and Mike Halford were advised by the security bureau in Nancheng that now was the time for them to depart for Hong Kong. The Sisters in the community were Sisters Baptist, Attracta, Berchmans, Francis and Malachy. The orphans and the old folk whom the Sisters looked after were in tears at their departure and a big crowd escorted them to the bus station. We were close to tears ourselves because we owed so much to the Sisters. With their departure the break-up of the Nancheng Diocese had, we realised bitterly, now really begun. I missed Mike Halford very much too. He was great fun and a great man to have around during 'liberation'.

Some time earlier, the military had informed the bishop that they would move into his house once the Sisters had departed and that we could live in the house vacated by the Sisters. It was a much smaller house, not big enough to accommodate all the priests who were in Nancheng at this time, but we could have been worse off. We were allowed to take our personal property of bedding and books. Over the years, Bishop Cleary had put together quite a sizeable library, ranging from theology, scripture, history, poetry to biographies and detective stories, and we transferred quite a selection of the books to the convent. The Reds told us we could store the rest of the books away in the attic of the Bishop's house and that they would be there for us whenever we wanted them. About a fortnight after we moved, Barney O'Neill and I returned for some of those books to discover that the Reds had taken most of them away. We were shocked and saddened to see how dirty the house had become and to note the extent it had deteriorated in the two weeks since we left. The old grandfather clock was stopped and the place seemed to be full of ghosts – ghosts of the priests whose home it had been when China was free. One seemed to hear the shuffle of their footsteps along the corridor and the ring of their laughter.

Towards the end of April, Seamus O'Reilly, on the Bishop's advice, came in from Chuliang parish to Nancheng in the Southern Line. Land Reform was starting in his place and he was having a lot of trouble, he told us. He added that the Reds had assured him they would not take over his house but we were not inclined to put much trust in their promises. They had taken over all the other parishes in the county. Pat Sheehy came in about the same time from Luki, the farthest away parish in the Northern Line and he had a more gloomy tale to tell. The Reds were making his life as miserable as they could. He was unable to get money through and had to live on a starvation diet. Since his house had been taken over by the local Reds, he was living in the sacristy of the church, a pokey, unheated room. He had spent at least one day in the jail in Luki.

After pondering the problem at some length, the Bishop decided to apply for exit visas for Vincent McNally and me, as we were criminals and therefore a liability. Subsequently, he decided to apply for visas for Barney O'Neill and Tom Fisher and to have another try at getting a visa for Mick Moran. This meant that he would just keep Pat Sheehy and Seamus as neither of them had any crimes.

The Sisters' convent and the orphanage etc., was a compound within the Catholic compound. Now, since the Sisters left, it had become a military compound and whereas the Bishop had been jailer for us criminals before, the military were really our jailers now. House arrest became a sort of military imprisonment. A number of armed military personnel guarded and lived in the buildings vacated by the Sisters and we were their prisoners. We had to try to adapt to a new situation and survive at the same time. The heart of the problem was that we could not get any money from either Shanghai or Hong Kong and that, at the same time, we feared we would be held responsible for the orphans and the old people who lived in the compound into which we were now moving. Catholic orphanages throughout China were very much in the news all that spring and demonstrations were held up and down the country in protest against the cruelty suffered by the orphans run by the Catholic Church. Of course, we realised immediately that this was a propaganda move and a subtle one to discredit the Catholic Church. The people who read the communist papers, however, saw it differently.

They saw that on February 28th, 1951, the communist papers accused the Canadian nuns of the congregation of the Immaculate Conception of criminal negligence in the case of the Holy Infant Foundling Home in Canton. Reports claimed that 94% of the babies received at the home during the past year had been killed by the nuns. It was alleged that babies had been starved and bitten to death by rats and that the nuns did nothing to protect the infants from mosquito bites. It was also reported that the older children in such orphanages had been exploited, that the well water in the

compound was unfit to drink and the children lived amid inde-
scribably unsanitary conditions while the nuns lived in luxury. The
papers also said that the children were so terrified of the nuns that
they had refused to speak to strangers in their presence.

Chinese newspapers nationwide took up the story and attacked the
missionary nuns. Editorial comment was followed by news from
different areas.

A series of protest meetings were held in Canton and Beijing and in
other towns up and down the country. An exhibition of pictures
showing alleged acts of cruelty by Catholic missionaries was held
in Canton. Large posters depicting nuns beating children and even
torturing them were shown all over the country and indeed, if I
remember correctly, in Nancheng. The nuns in Canton were paraded
through the streets, stoned, spat upon and subjected to many indignities. The 'trial', like the charges brought against the Sisters, was a
farce, but it was conducted with a degree of barbarism generally
associated with the Roman amphitheatres according to a Sword of
the Spirit pamphlet called 'Religious Freedom in Red China'.

CHAPTER 14

The Faith of Kiutu

The Kiutu people, my people, were in the news and had been in the news for the past three weeks. We were getting all kinds of rumours about the number of Kiutu Catholics who had apostatised under merciless pressure from the Commissar. One figure put it as high as two-thirds. Looking back now, I think that these few weeks were the most nerve-wrecking that I had experienced since the communists took over.

Then about the second week in February, Thoni came in to see me and told me what had happened. Here is the full story:

The Commissar in Kiutu had summoned the people to the church the day after I was expelled. He had lit the candles on the altar, and the sanctuary lamp, in mockery. Then he ascended the pulpit and told the people, many of whom were crying, that I had been expelled because I was a criminal, not because I was a Catholic priest. Said he, 'You call him Sen Fu – I call him criminal Tien.'

After the meeting, he donned the benediction cope and walked through the village derisively asking the people to call him Sen Fu. He then cut up the wooden altars, took them out of the church and used them as dining tables. Later he and his agents took out the baptismal font and used it as a pigs' trough. The empty tabernacle was used as a nest for setting hens. All the sacred vessels and sacred objects were taken away from the church and Wang Gee Poo had a ladder and proceeded to take the glass from the Stations of the Cross and take down the stations, but he fell from the top of the ladder and hurt himself. Tai Yang warned him that God was punishing him but he took no notice of her. They made garments of one kind or another from the linen and cloth that they found in the sacristy. The Commissar's elder son, about ten years old, was wearing my surplice as an everyday garb and one of his playthings was the relic of Blessed Gabriel Perboyre CM. In the sanctuary of the church there was a painting of our Blessed Lady by a Chinese artist – a Chinese Madonna. Beneath the picture, and to the sides of it, on slabs of rare Chinese wood, done in elegant Chinese characters, were titles of Our Blessed Lady from the Litany, titles like 'Help of Christians', 'Comfort of the Afflicted', etc. The titles were placed there to honour Our Blessed Mother. The communists took the slabs of wood bearing Our Lady's titles from the sanctuary and nailed them on the village lavatory and when the distressed Catholics tried to take away Our Lady's titles, they were prevented by armed soldiers. Whenever I think of this incident, a line of a hymn we learned as children comes to mind, and the line is 'When wicked men blaspheme thee, we will love and bless thy name.' Certainly they were misguided men.

But the Commissar did not confine himself to profaning the sacred. Two weeks later he assembled the Catholics again, upbraided them for not making accusations against me and to their horror, told them that none of them would get any land unless they renounced their faith. With him, all ready for signatures, he had a formula of apostasy. This document stated that the Catholic Church was the tool of Imperialism, and that Imperialism was now overthrown. Hence patriotic Chinese should renounce their allegiance to the Church and the Pope, and follow Mao Tse Tung.

This unexpected ultimatum placed the Catholics in a cruel dilemma. Most of them were so poor, and they could only afford meat on big Feast days and at the Chinese New Year. The land they were promised would provide them with better food and clothing. For Chinese of their class, land was life. So the temptation was most severe. To add to the severity, the Commissar assembled them pretty well each day for three weeks and put tremendous pressure on them to take the land.

When after three weeks the Commissar abandoned his policy of forcing the Catholics to apostatise (he abandoned his policy because he had failed and was running behind schedule in the Land division programme), only then did the truth emerge. In all about six families had renounced their faith. Some had been lapsed Catholics, some had been puppets of the Commissar. In every case, it was the husband who had signed and, in most cases, the women had disclaimed responsibility for their husband's actions. The

Commissar, in the first few days of assembly, thought he would stampede quite a few people into signing by bullying tactics.

Then the Yu tribe held a meeting. Most of the Catholics belonged to that tribe. 'Dead with the Hunger' was a Yu, so was Shin Faih, the carpenter and Mi Fung, the sister of Fr Tommy Yu and Sr Teresita Yu, a Columban Sister. But the meeting was not confined to the Yu clan. The hard core of last ditch Catholics - and there were many of them - attended. At the meeting, all present decided that they would never sign the document or renounce their faith. This decision they conveyed to the other Catholics, and it gave courage to the latter to persevere. 'Dead with the Hunger' went further and issued a statement himself. He said, 'You call me "Dead with the Hunger", and I know I look the part. I am now sixty years old, and all my life I have been starving. I have never had enough rice to tide me over more than three months of the year. Most of my life is now gone and I am not going to sign away my faith in order that I may have enough rice for the rest of it.' The six householders who did sign the document had more rice for the next year than they ever had in the past. Only for the next year though, because all the land in the area, ironically enough, was given over to the military in 1951. The Chinese stepped up their aid to the communists in Korea at that time, and large tracts of land were requisitioned for the military towards this end. When the military got the land, all the villagers were supplied with ration cards. They had to queue up at the village rice granary to get their ration of rice. In fairness, it should be said that the communists told the people before Land Division that collectivisation, when the State would own all the land, was their aim. Giving land to poor people was just a temporary measure. So, long term, the 144 families who gave such heroic witness did as well materially as the six households who had signed the document.

As far as I know, Kiutu was the only place in our area where the communists tried to make Catholics apostatise under threat of giving them no land. But then our Commissar showed exceptional zeal in suppressing the Church and stamping out all vestiges of the sacred. Shortly before I was expelled, he told Tai Yang he had apostatised fifteen years earlier in Hubei, and that his parents were still Catholics. Tai Yang passed on the information to me. Though she held on to her faith when poor Shay Yung renounced hers, she still had to work for the Reds. Some of the Catholics came to me and said, 'Don't trust Tai Yang, she may be a communist agent.' The fact is, she was our agent. As the communists stepped up the persecution, she kept me informed step by step to the best of her ability. I never expected she would play such a valiant part, as she was only a recent convert. She died a few years ago.

The poor Commissar! Perhaps the tenacity with which the local Catholics held on to their faith jolted him into reconsidering his position. The meetings of the last ditch Catholics and 'Dead with the Hunger's' statement must have infuriated him, but impressed him too. Infuriated him, because the meeting was held in defiance of the Commissar's orders, and because the statement contained a humorous but veiled barb aimed at the Commissar and his Marxist materialism. Impressed, because he was powerless to do anything about it. At the meeting there were many poor (the people he had come to liberate) and 'Dead with the Hunger' was the ranking pauper. 'Dead with the Hunger's witness was very quotable. The people would be looking for a laugh in it. They got it, and the laugh was on the Commissar.

It is not always the people you expect will give outstanding witness in persecution who give it. I would have expected the hard core of first class Catholics to rally the people who wavered. They lived up to my expectations. I would not have thought 'Dead with the Hunger' would have played so effective a role. He was no fanatic for going to church. He had misunderstandings with the former pastor. But his loyalty to the Faith, and to the Church ran deep.

We were all thrilled when we heard of the heroic witness given by the Kiutu Catholics. We were filled with hope for the future, too, hope that other parishes would be inspired by their lead when persecution came to them. Listening to Thoni tell of the Kiutu experience, I realised, I suppose for the first time, how violently Our Lord and his Church are hated. And it was a distressing experience. But the story also brought home to me, when I heard of the resistance of the Kiutu people, how deeply Our Lord and his Church are loved and I felt full of joy and gratitude.

Thoni sprung another pleasant surprise on me. He told me that he would like to become a priest and asked me to help him. He had been to me a very loyal and helpful friend and he was bright and full of humour. He had suffered because he was helping me and helping the church and, of course, Wang Gee Poo had threatened to put him in jail a few times if he didn't apostatise. He had seen the church going through its agony and realised that the agony was only starting, yet still he wanted to be a priest. I felt so grateful to God, but I consulted Bishop Cleary and he was very interested. He said that in Shaowu, in Fujian Province, south of our diocese, Monsignor Koenig, a German Salvatorian, had still a junior seminary. Apparently Max Koenig, as we called him, did not have much trouble in Shaowu since the Reds took over. Some of our priests had helped the Salvatorians when they were interned during the war and Pat Dermody, Mike Halford and Mark Kelly were three of these priests, so we knew them fairly well. I wrote to Max and he said he would be very pleased to accept Thoni but, at the moment, he wasn't taking new students. He was waiting until he saw how Land Division went in his area. However, some months later the communists started to bolshevise Fujian and the Salvatorian Seminary was closed down and Thoni was unable to study for the priesthood.

CHAPTER 15

The Heat of the Sun

When we moved into our new quarters and realised that we were responsible for the orphanage, we did a lot of soul searching. Seeing that we couldn't get any money from either Hong Kong or Shanghai, we would be unable to pay the staff who looked after the orphans when the Sisters were running the orphanage. With all the hullabaloo about Catholic orphanages in the papers, we were afraid that if we closed down the orphanage, the Reds might use it as an opportunity to discredit the church locally, and expel all of us at once. The bishop did not want this and I don't think any of us did either. But the bishop had now to think about the four seminarians we had with us and about the Chinese priests, and about how he could help them in the time left to him. We had a meeting about the matter and it was obvious that the bishop badly wanted to buy time. So we decided to buy time for him by doing the manual work which the staff who looked after the orphanage did when the Sisters were with us. Fortunately, we had a good stock of rice in the granary and we did own, I suppose, about ten pigs.

In organising our project, our aim was a bit like that enunciated in 'The Peter Principle' - a funny book on industry and incompetence etc. According to the book, in business and industry, there should be a 'slot for every clot' on the pay-roll. We did not have a pay-roll, but we did have a number of slots to be filled. I can assure you, when the jobs were dished out, this clot did not land a very prestigious slot. I was only given the task of cutting firewood and drawing water, and Pat Sheehy got the same kind of job. Seamus O'Reilly and Tom Fisher cooked vegetables and rice for the pigs and for all the people, Chinese and foreign, in the compound. The bishop's slot was a lowly one. He swept the floors. Mick Moran, on the other hand, landed the most prestigious portfolio of pig supremo and some of us felt a little envious when we saw him move into action.

If somebody told us that we would survive a Nancheng summer doing manual labour in the open, day by day, we would not have believed them. But God, who 'tempers the wind to the shorn lamb' can put blinkers on the sun to save the half-starved missionary and the last week of July and the beginning of August was cooler than the previous two years.

And then, early in August the visas for which the bishop had applied for a number of us missionaries were granted. There was only one refusal and that was Mick Moran.So busy were we trying to survive, trying to buy time for the bishop, and trying to keep the orphans and old people alive, that we had almost forgotten about the visas. I felt rather sorry about the prospect of leaving because, for one thing, the Kiutu Catholics had been coming in during the week-days and I had been able to hear their confessions and give them Holy Communion privately. Quite a large number of them managed to come during the summer months and it was possible to exercise a restricted, but nonetheless, real apostolate in regard to them. The armed military guards were not strict in admitting very poorly dressed people into the compound. The shrewd Catholics would come, not in their Sunday best, but in their weekday worst. Admittedly, it was a tenuous contact, but all the more precious for that very reason. The Kiutu people who visited me were quite disillusioned by the consequences of the land division. They had been promised that the spoils taken from the landlords would be handed over to the poor. In practice, what happened in the district was that the communists robbed the rich in the name of the poor but the Party and the army shared all but token amounts between themselves.

And then, on the afternoon of August 8th, the date that the visas were granted to us, we were sitting round after tiffin when a messenger from the Commissar's office arrived. Jim Yang took the note, opened it and, looking sadly at me, said, 'I'm sorry, Luke, your visa, though granted by the local authorities in Nancheng, has been cancelled by a higher authority.' Presumably it was the Provincial Governor in Nanchang who refused it.

I cannot say I was sorry for myself for the reasons I have given, but one man who was really happy at the news was Mick Moran. He had been hurt when the Reds had singled him out for refusal but now that my request for a visa was also turned down there were two of us in the same boat and he felt much better about things.

On the Feast of the Assumption I was overjoyed to see nearly a hundred Catholics from Kiutu to celebrate the feast. They had so many things to tell me and I had so many questions to ask them that the time they were in Nancheng passed all too quickly. They had fully outgrown the effects of the indoctrination given during the hate campaign that prefaced Land Reform. They spoke with sympathy of the poor landlords and with disgust of the Commissar.

After Mass on that same day, Barney O'Neill, Tom Fisher, Vincent McNally and Pat Sheehy, left by bus for Hong Kong.

The Catholics from Nancheng escorted Barney and Tom to the bus station and some of Vincent's Catholics from Hsiao Shih came to see him off.

For days after their departure the house which they had left behind seemed terribly empty, the days seemed to drag and the nights were worst of all. Often as I sat in my room at night I could hear the voices of my departed friends raised in song and laughter. The light of other days lingered round us. 'Every parting is a foretaste of death and every reunion, a foretaste of the resurrection.'

PART III:

Leaving China

CHAPTER 16

Patriotism in Church

By this time, we had become experts at adapting ourselves to new situations. Now that we were no longer responsible for the old people or the orphans, the bishop gave all his time to the Chinese priests, and to the four seminarians. Joseph Peng had only a year's theology to do and he would have his course finished and could be ordained. The other three seminarians, Tommy Yu, Joseph Wu, Peter Hsieh, were just starting theology. The bishop, in his humourous way, reminded me that I had been a some-time professor and would I mind having another bash. Again, there was a 'slot for every clot' and the bishop and Jim Yang and Seamus got the other slots. I took Joe Peng, who was within a year of ordination, for moral and pastoral theology and the other three seminarians for something else. We realised by now, that we were not training seminarians to pass examinations but to witness in persecution, and that realisation made the job easier and helped us to make our teaching more relevant. Another thing that helped me was a letter I had from Mike Halford. He told me he was already a professor in a Columban College in Boston. His technique, he said, was to keep two jumps ahead of the boys and he found this of assistance.

All through late summer and early autumn, the Nuncio Archbishop Riberi got big coverage in the communist newspaper. The paper denounced him as an Imperialist and called for his expulsion. On September 4th, the day the Nuncio was expelled, there appeared in the People's Daily, an editorial defining freedom of religion and saying it applied only to churches which had no ties with imperialism, so in Nancheng they said they were starting an anti-imperialistic patriotic church movement.

To pioneer the movement in Nancheng, the Reds selected the former headmaster of our primary school, a man who had firmly refused to apostatise a year earlier and had defended the Catholic position against all comers. I do not know how they wore down the poor man eventually. Perhaps they tried flattery and appealed to his patriotism. I do know they sought his company and invited him to their social affairs and then we heard he was appointed to the Board of Directors of the Catholic hospital. The headmaster's prestige grew apace and so did his desire to serve his country.

A training course was scheduled for the hospital staff early in September. The hospital, I should explain, had been taken over several months before and we were in financial straits because of Government restrictions on getting money into China. No compensation had been offered for the medical equipment and supplies; on the contrary, a huge subsidy for a grandiose development scheme was demanded. The bishop refused and the Reds let the matter rest for the moment. Many members of the hospital staff were Catholics and we were left in the dark about what was happening to them during the indoctrination sessions. Lectures were given by the headmaster, assisted by a few Red propagandists from party headquarters. These went on for about a month. A hate campaign was brewing, we concluded, when we noticed that nurses and orderlies refused to look in Mick Moran's direction, let alone speak to him. I personally realised how fast things were moving when one of the nurses, Er Nu, stopped speaking to me. She was a lovely girl and her father, Wong Gin Tin, was a catechist and I knew him well.

Then, without warning, another blow fell. A note from the Mandarin's office on the 2nd October informed Mick Moran that he was to appear in the People's court at 3 o'clock that same day. This would be his third trial. We wished him luck and, accompanied by Seamus O'Reilly, he set off for the court.

The trial was held in a theatre. The preliminaries had just begun when a stout frightened man, a landlord in the old days, was brought in in chains and placed beside Mick. Both men were ordered to stand on small stools so that all could see them. Mick was not allowed to speak. The Mandarin and the accusers did all the talking. One of the most aggressive spokesmen for the prosecution was unfortunately Teacher Dong, one of Mick's teachers who had apostatised. The mob clamoured for the death penalty for the two accused.

The trial lasted for two hours and a 'Chan-pai' (execution tablet) bearing the death sentence was thrust round the tattered jacket of the landlord. He was rudely pushed off the stool, falling head first, as his hands and feet were bound. A roar of laughter went up from the spectators. Mick Moran's sentence was not announced. He was helped off the stool and led off with the landlord. The court then broke up.

Anxiously Seamus made his way through the body of the court to where the Mandarin was sitting and enquired what Mick's sentence was? 'Find out at the police station,' snapped the Mandarin. Knowing that that was all the information he could get, Seamus returned to the mission alone.

Shortly after Seamus came back to us, a messenger arrived from the police station to inform us that Mick was spending the night in jail and that he would be expelled the following morning. The messenger offered to take food and the luggage needed for the journey to Mick. We gave him some food and a small bag containing a Breviary, a change of clothes and shaving kit.

Thus, without a goodbye, our ranking criminal was lost to our little company of hemmed-in Columbans. I thought it remarkable that he was escorted out of China on the feast of St Thérèse, Patroness of the Foreign Missions, to whom he had great devotion.

Shortly afterwards, Bishop Charlie Quinn (any missionary ten years in China could call him Charlie!) and two of his priests were expelled from Yukiang. The 'crimes and expulsion' of Archbishop Riberi, the Nuncio, provided subject matter for many sessions in the training course which was now well under way in the hospital in Nancheng. The headmaster still maintained that he was a Catholic, but that as a patriot he joined the protest initiated by the Reds against the Archbishop. He showed how the Archbishop was really the leader of an imperialistic spy ring. At first he was magnanimous enough to admit that Bishop Cleary would not do anything like that and that patriotic Chinese should not judge other bishops by the crimes of Archbishop Riberi.

Up to this time kid-glove methods had been used by the local Red Propaganda Office but now our doctor attended one of the training courses and informed the hospital staff that unless they joined the group, whose object was to set up a Patriotic Anti-Imperialist Church, they would definitely lose their jobs in the hospital and that no jobs would be available to them in any other medical centre. They could if they wished, of course, go to the hills and cut firewood. Terrified by this threat, every member of the staff joined the study group except one old man called Jacoby.

They joined this although they knew at the time that the ultimate aim of the study group was to trump up charges against the bishop, expel him from China and to start a schismatic church. To promote this ultimate aim, the headmaster, the doctor and their helpers approached the weakest of the Catholics and those who had grievances, real or imaginary, against the Church or the bishop. From these, they attempted to form another nucleus which would further the cause of the Patriotic Church amongst the rank and file. I do not know at what stage the doctor joined the headmaster in the campaign against the local church or bishops.

Such was the state of affairs in Nancheng when Con O'Connell and Pat Gately passed through, on their way to Hong Kong, about the end of October. They had been stationed in Kwang Chang, about a hundred and twenty miles south from Nancheng, in the Nanfeng area. They had been under house arrest for a year and a half and had suffered untold minor torments from the Reds; the latter had forbidden the people to come to church shortly after the liberation, and both priests had been tried on more than one occasion. But their big worry was the middle-school students whom the Reds unleashed on them to abuse and blackguard them, sometimes every day and sometimes once a week. One of their most original tricks was to get two ladders and place them against the windows of the priest's bedrooms. Then very early in the morning they would get two girls from the middle school and ask them to climb up the ladders to the windows of the bedrooms. Then they would collect the towns-people and point out to them the girls were descending from the priests' rooms. They would tell the girls to stand at the top of the ladders until photographers would come and take pictures. Then the Red leaders would urge the people to condemn the foreign law-breakers and punish them as seducers of the young. Finally, they were expelled.

Pat Gately did not suffer as much as one would have expected. He was an American and most of the Americans in the neighbouring dioceses had been treated much worse than he was. Apart from us, who were still in Nancheng, Con O'Connell and Pat Gately were the last two Columbans to leave the diocese. After they had left, we felt now that the Reds had really rolled up the diocese as one rolls up a carpet.

Since the summer, our fare had been very poor and we were still unable to get any money and could only manage a couple of ounces of meat a week. Part of the time we were strictly vegetarian. Then one day we noticed that the dog had disappeared. He was a grey fuzzy-haired mongrel, near to the terrier type. At lunch we were surprised when Peter Hsieh, the seminarian, who was now doing our cooking, brought in a dish of meat and invited us to 'cha gao' which interpreted means 'eat dog'. The meat tasted well enough and although it was a little tough and dry, it saved us from the stigma of vegetarianism for a few days. Dog and snails we could manage fairly well, but when off-season turtles began to make their appearance on the menu, we became a little fastidious. Some of the Catholics provided us with a very pleasant surprise and brought us chicken for St Columban's Day which we celebrated in a more subdued fashion than in former years.

Every night in the hospital the training courses were going apace. The Reds brow-beat and urged the Chinese priests to attend these meetings. Every night, as I visited the Blessed Sacrament in the chapel, I could hear them abusing the Church and its ministers. I do not think I ever felt as downcast in my life as during that period – to think that the hospital staff, many of whom had been educated, all of whom had been befriended in a special way by the Church, were now working frantically to undermine and destroy the Church of which they were the children.

Early in December, it transpired that there was, as well as the doctor and the headmaster, another leader from the hospital who, with them, was actively engaged in starting a schismatic church. Things had gone so far that the bishop felt in conscience that he had to excommunicate the leaders. This he did, about the middle of December. As well as excommunicating three ringleaders, he also pointed out that the charges made against Fr Moran were all false. Further, he informed the congregation that ordinary Catholics who had joined the Patriotic Church Movement could not receive absolution until they promised to leave the Movement. The bishop also emphasised that the Legion of Mary was not an imperialistic movement, but that it was a Church society. Seamus O'Reilly and Jim Yang reiterated the bishop's remarks in their sermons.

The ringleaders were hopping mad when they heard they were excommunicated. The headmaster came to the bishop in the afternoon and demanded an explanation and asked for a copy of the sermon. The bishop pointed out the gravity of the headmaster's attacks on the Church. He recalled to him how a year earlier he had defended the Church during the training course and how proud we were of him then. He exhorted him to abandon the Patriotic Church Movement and rally round the Catholic Church of which he had been a member. 'Of course, they will put you in jail if you do that,' said the bishop, 'but you will be much happier than you are now.' The headmaster, however, just turned away sulkily and promised nothing.

A few days later, I was standing outside the convent church, about two o'clock in the afternoon, when Tommy Yu, one of our seminarians, rushed up to me and whispered, 'One of the nurses at the hospital has reported that you refused her absolution this morning; she said you refused it because she had joined the Patriotic Church Movement. The communists have heard about this and there will be probably serious repercussions.' When I told the bishop about it, he said, 'That's a good thing. It is the first shot across their bows; they may put us out of the country as a result.' That evening, Jim Yang told us that the headmaster, fuming with anger, had accosted him. The teacher and one of his henchmen had threatened that they would beat and kick me. 'Well,' said I, 'I shall be going down to ring the Angelus Bell tomorrow and we shall see what happens.' 'I'd like to see them try to beat you up,' said Seamus. The next day, as I passed the dispensary, the headmaster looked daggers at me and all the nurses looked in the opposite direction when they saw me. Nothing more drastic than that happened.

Of course, we realised that the headmaster and his companions were still smarting under the bishop's excommunication pronouncement and that they were planning a speedy revenge. I heard they would cause trouble at the Christmas midnight Mass, so the bishop decided not to have a midnight Mass.

Then, on Christmas Eve, 1951, around midday, Seamus brought us the most intriguing and improbable-sounding of rumours. The rumour going the rounds was that the National Patriotic Church leaders planned to seize the pulpit on Christmas Day during Bishop Cleary's Mass. They hoped to terrify the people by having Red police stationed at strategic points in the Cathedral and armed soldiers at the three doors. From the pulpit one of them would address the people on the Patriotic Church Movement and try to enlist new members. They would impress on Catholics that by joining their Patriotic Church they still would be members of their own church, the Catholic Church. More importantly, such people would be Patriotic Catholics, recognising not the Pope but the helmsman, Mao Tse Tung himself, as head of the Patriotic Church in China.

Our first instinct was to discount the rumour. Our reason was that, like Kiutu, Nancheng was one of the most fertile rumour-producing belts in that part of South China. Yet, the more we reviewed the events of the previous few weeks, round high noon that Christmas Eve, the more likely it seemed that something dramatic would be staged by the Patriotic Church during the season of peace and good will.

At tiffin, that Christmas Eve, I noticed Bishop Cleary was unusually silent as he polished off his bowl of rice. Ordinarily he liked a bit of banter and repartee with his priests and loved to get as good as he gave. Today, however, his eyes were raised somewhat, his head cast back a little, like a man who is trying to decide which card to play next. When he had finished his bowl of rice, he joined our conversation and said, 'If the leaders of the Patriotic Church and their satellites seize the pulpit, we'll get the people to sing the Rosary and drown down the eloquence of our "guest speakers".' A Celtic twinkle came into his blue laughing eyes as he continued, 'You boys, lead them at the rosary (actually the Chinese always sang the Rosary but never at Mass) and keep on no matter what happens. We cannot resist them physically but prayerful resistance will be more effective.'

When Seamus and I entered the Cathedral on Christmas morning, about half past seven, it did not look like 'a house of prayer' but a den of Reds. The place was nearly half full of communist propaganda officials, police, members of the Patriotic Church, and armed soldiers at the three doors. Seamus and I started to hear confessions at the two side doors and a Chinese priest was hearing at the altar rails. The air was electric with tension when the bishop started Mass. As I looked sideways to the front door, who did I see coming in but a big crowd of my own parishioners. They had walked over ten miles through the mud and slush even though they had been threatened with severe penalties if they attempted the journey, by their local Commissar in Kiutu. I was overjoyed to see them and they flocked around me for confession

As the bishop was about to finish reading the Gospel at the altar, a spokesman for the Patriotic Church got into the pulpit and started to address the people in a very loud voice. He said he was going to speak to them on the new Anti-Imperialist Patriotic Church and asked them to 'lend him an ear'. Far from 'lending an ear', they lent him their voices and started to sing the Rosary with full-throated gusto. The louder he shouted, the louder they sang. 'Shin er de Malia, Mon Pay Shin dung Da', 'Hail Mary full of grace'. Soon Seamus was on his feet boldly urging the people on the Gospel side to keep up the volume.

In the ancient world, no matter how you felt, the Greeks had a word for it, we are told. In the modern world, it's the Americans, and the way I felt that morning was 'cop-shy'. I felt cop-shy because there were so many policemen in the church, so many soldiers, so many officers of the Patriotic Church Movement, and they had read of my crimes in the papers and saw the cartoons depicting these crimes in the city hoardings. That morning, I felt like a criminal – not every inch a criminal, maybe every other inch, and felt the albatross back around my neck for the first time since Mike Halford visited me in Kiutu. The albatross seemed to weigh nearly a ton. Still, when I had finished the confession I was hearing I got up, explained to my waiting parishioners where I was going and exhorted them to sing their heads off. Then I started to 'conduct the choir' on the Epistle side (as we called it then) and the response was loud and high from tenors, baritones, bass profundos... the lot. As I approached the altar rails, I could see I had run into a spot of trouble. The Chinese priest, Jim Yang, who was hearing confessions, was being blackguarded by a member of the Patriotic Church called Shung Bay Tai, an orderly in the hospital. The latter was listening to what the penitent – an old lady – had been confessing, and generally making a mockery of the sacrament, despite the protest of

Jim Yang. So I just grabbed Shung Bay Tai very gently by the collar of his Sun Yat Sen coat (the type of coat worn by the late Mao Tse Tung and his followers), pulled him away from the altar rails and even more gently still said to him, 'This is a sacrament that is being administered.'

Although it was all done so gently, he was not a bit pleased at my intervention. In fact, he was furious and shouted at the top of his voice, 'Mo da nin chia', meaning 'Do not be striking me'. The guest speaker stopped. The choir stopped. Silence broke out all through the Cathedral and into the vacuum I automatically intoned my response. 'Shin gow yu tzu', 'There is freedom of religion.' This was a quotation from the Communist Constitution of October 1949 and it was a reflex action on my part.

At this, the guest speaker left the pulpit and came rushing towards me but to my great surprise he passed me by. The singing re-started because another guest speaker had gone into the pulpit. His words were greeted with a vocal barrage from the choir which even surpassed their performance before the interval. The man who had gone into the pulpit was the doctor mentioned earlier.

When the headmaster, the leader who had left the pulpit, failed to stop the singing in the church, he took out his notebook and started to take the names of the singers. Some of them got frightened and stopped singing. When I saw this, I followed him down the Epistle side and exhorted the people to pray again as praying was not a crime. And again they burst into song. On the Gospel side, under Seamus's expert conducting, the people were singing fortissimo all the time.

When the headmaster and I met, he was coming up towards the altar writing names in his notebook – I was going in the opposite direction, urging them to keep singing – the people found themselves in a dilemma. Some of them solved it by a brilliant compromise. They did not sing and thus kept their names out of the notebook but they did say the Hail Mary with their lips and Our Lady, who is 'Help of the half-defeated' heard their prayers that Christmas morning and strengthened them in their faith and fortitude. Gradually, the Catholics grew more confident, ignored the headmaster's notebook, and guest speaker number two left the pulpit and joined his fellow preacher outside the church. Bishop Cleary continued his Mass, the people sang the Mass prayers in Chinese and Seamus and I started hearing confessions again. At the Communion, the Patriotic Church group took down the names of the 291 people who received Holy Communion that morning.

After Mass, I had the delightful experience of talking to seventy people from my parish individually. They had come in bravely for the feast, undeterred by police, soldiers and other officials. Their smiles often intermingled with their tears, their laughter with their weeping, as they gave me the latest news from the parish. When I congratulated them on the heroic witness they had given during the persecution a year earlier, they gave thanks to God and took no credit for themselves. For me, the parting was painful because I did not know if ever I would see these magnificent people again.

As the Kiutu people were leaving, a tall stout Nancheng man, who I think had joined the communist Party, came up to take me to the police station. I told him that he had no right and that I would not go along with him. I also told him I had already been arrested a few times by the People's Army of Liberation. Seeing that we were held prisoners in their military compound by the same army of liberation, I felt arresting me again would be overdoing it somewhat. Then he was joined by some members of the Patriotic Church Movement and they were all insisting that I be taken to the police station and that I come along with them at once. I refused to go and when Seamus heard the altercation, he rushed up and told the crowd that they had no right to apprehend me and that they should go home at once as he had to close the door of the cathedral.

Tiffin was a very joyful meal that Christmas Day. Bishop Cleary was thrilled at the way the Catholics had shown their mettle under pressure and felt their morale had been boosted immensely as a result. He was something of a Peter Pan and, though in his late sixties, he was full of boyish glee at the way his plan worked out. Boyish is the operative word, and I have never seen him in such boyish high spirits as during that meal. As I have already said he was a very good listener, and encouraged others, especially young priests, to air their views, and share their jokes. But this Christmas Day was an exception. His comments, jokes, followed each other in quick succession. Of course, from the sanctuary, he had a better view of the 'proceedings' in the body of the church than we priests enjoyed, and though his observations were very funny, they showed understanding and compassion.

On the feast of the Epiphany, 1952, the Catholic Patriotic Committee was established. It issued a manifesto denouncing the Imperialistic Church and the autocratic manner in which the bishop and the priests treated the Nancheng Catholics. Then they sought signatures for the manifesto and set up an office in the church and another in the town where people could come and sign their names. They announced that Catholics were free to sign or not to sign but they also informed them that if they did not sign, terrible consequences would ensue. They roped in the local police and the Farmers Association to help them 'persuade' the people to sign.

Then the Patriotic Church formed a second committee consisting of six men and six women. The twelve of them were weak Catholics who had joined the Patriotic Church earlier. The 'Twelve Apostles', as they were called, summoned a meeting of all the Catholics in the parish and the meeting was held in the Cathedral on the 10th of January. It was attended by the county Commissar and this was the first time that he publicly showed his interest in the Patriotic Church Movement. He besought the assembly to be patriotic and join the Patriotic Church. Those who signed the manifesto were regarded as members of the Patriotic Church. Many refused, but a fair number signed.

By now, the bishop was wondering if his denunciation of the Patriotic Church and its promoters had been fully understood and he feared that the people did not appreciate the danger of the new movement. So he asked Jim Yang to preach another sermon on the Sunday within the Octave of the Epiphany. I was sitting at the back of the church while he was preaching. Jim told me beforehand that he felt this sermon would be his last, and would indeed be his death-warrant. In the pulpit he explained to the people the nature of and the danger of the new movement and exhorted them to hold fast to their Catholic faith. He told them that he certainly would have to suffer himself for having preached this sermon and he asked for their prayers. It was a most impressive performance and by the time he came to the end of the sermon, most of the Catholics were in tears.

When the headmaster and his helpers heard about Jim Yang's sermon, they were enraged and started to put much heavier pressure on the ordinary Catholics to join the Movement than they had done in the past. Day by day, rumours were coming in of the large numbers who had joined the Movement. Of course, one could never be sure of the credibility of such rumours.

On the second Sunday of the Epiphany, Jim Yang was summoned to the office of the county Commissar. We all felt that this was the end of the road for Jim Yang and that he was certainly being summoned on account of the sermon he had preached a fortnight earlier. We were full of forebodings that we would never see him again.

After tiffin, that particular day, all of us priests went to the bishop's room where he talked to Jim Yang for a few minutes. Jim Yang knelt down and asked the bishop for his blessing. The bishop solemnly blessed him and said, 'God bless you. Trust in Our Blessed Lady. You have a good chance of being shot. When they take you out to shoot you, sing the Divine Praises. You will be a martyr no matter how they twist it.' We then walked along the corridor to the point where the communist soldiers were waiting for him. The bishop and Jim Yang walked together and then John Chang and I followed them and we were followed by Seamus O'Reilly and Paul Yu. I remember well what John Dhong said to me as we walked along in that small but solemn procession. He said 'Shou nan shi women ti shin tao' which means 'Suffering is our vocation'. Poor man, he had suffered a lot from tuberculosis since he was a seminarian and now he was under heavy stress and strain as the persecution hotted up.

Contrary to all expectations, Jim Yang came back to the church a couple of hours later and provided us with the most pleasant of surprises. The Commissar at first threatened, then coaxed him to join the Patriotic Church Movement. Jim steadfastly refused and the Commissar got very angry and said, 'If that's your mentality, you know what is in store for you. After you are dead, the people will spit on your grave.' 'History will vindicate me,' said Jim with some defiance. Later the same day, John Chang was called down to the Commissar's office and questioned about the Legion of Mary. He was willing to give the names to the Commissar because the latter already knew them. The Commissar, however, wanted him to sign a document to the effect that he had discontinued the Legion and he refused to do this, feeling that the Commissar would twist his words in the statement.

A few days later, around seven o'clock in the evening, I was summoned to the office of the Patriotic Church Movement. A representative of the Commissar, who was known to us as 'The Sage', started to interrogate me in loud arrogant tones. Said he, 'Last Sunday you refused to give absolution to a Catholic woman because she had joined the Patriotic Church Movement. This is against the law and we shall not stand for any violation of the law from you. You are sabotaging the Patriotic Church.' And then he went on to dilate on the seriousness of that crime.

When he had finished, I explained to him gently what the seal of confession implied and that therefore I was not free to discuss the matter any further with him. I did, however, point out that in hearing confessions I had been guided by the teachings of the Catholic Church and not by the orders of 'The Sage' or his fellow workers. This maddened him and he sneered in a low hissing voice, 'Imperialist'. I replied with a little animation, 'If you knew anything about history you would realise that we Irish are not imperialists and that we have suffered greatly from imperialism'. Then surprise, surprise, a communist from North China who was present said to 'The Sage', 'That is right, the Irish are not imperialists. They too, have become a republic – just a few years ago. They have suffered a lot from the imperialists.' The northerner wanted to show that he was better educated than 'The Sage', but his intervention defused the situation somewhat. After warning me that if I sabotaged the Patriotic Church Movement again, I would rue the consequences, they told me to return to the church.

About two weeks later, I started hearing confessions around seven o'clock in the Cathedral on a Sunday morning, when in comes 'The Sage' accompanied by an armed communist aide. He came up to the confessional and started to listen to what I was saying to the Catholic who was going to confession, holding his ear close to the slide. I stood up and told him to leave the church and not to violate Chairman Mao's law but he just pranced with rage and said it was I who was violating the law. He maintained that I was telling the penitent not to join the Patriotic Church Movement and that he had proof that I sabotaged the said Movement whenever a Catholic came to confession. By this time, the penitent had rushed away from the confessional in fright and 'The Sage' and his aide withdrew to the back door of the church. When later another Catholic came for confession, he again rushed up and put his ear to the slide and shouted in a loud voice, 'None of this sabotaging the Patriotic Church Movement!' I absolved the penitent quickly and told 'The Sage' that I would report him for interfering with our freedom of religion. He shouted at me again and told me he would take me to the police office immediately. It was just about consecration time in the Mass that was being said so I knelt down and ignored his summons. He continued shouting during the consecration and when it was over I accompanied him to the door. 'All right,' I said, 'I shall go with you to the police station but I shall report you.'

On the steps of the cathedral, 'The Sage' started to scold and reprove me but Seamus O'Reilly (he always seemed to turn up in the nick of time and save the situation) followed us out. He accused 'The Sage' of interfering with freedom of religion and 'The Sage' argued with him for a few minutes and then abandoned his plan of taking me to the police station. We entered the church again but 'The Sage' followed Seamus and me and for the rest of that morning very few Catholics dared to come to confession. The next Sunday they were also terrified. 'The Sage's' interference had frightened them and lowered their morale considerably.

CHAPTER 17

Before the People's Court

Towards the end of January, the Patriotic Church Group, having obtained quite a few signatures for their movement, set themselves another task. They sought amongst the weak Catholics for people who would trump up charges against the bishop and the priests. They worked hard at this for a couple of weeks. Then they put our crimes on paper and posted them in prominent parts of the city. All of this was in preparation for the big trial which was to take place early in February and there were many rumours as to what the outcome of this trial would be.

Most of the people thought that Jim Yang would be shot. They thought that our star catechist 'McCormack', who had been arrested a couple of months previously, and who had been continuing his apostolate in jail in spite of beatings and chains, would also be shot. It was expected that the bishop would be expelled immediately after the trial and that Seamus and I would receive a similar sentence. Later rumours had it that only the bishop would be expelled and that I would be given solitary confinement and that maybe Seamus would be allowed to stay in Nancheng. The trial was scheduled for February 8th.

The evening before I went over to the Cathedral to carry out my duties as verger for the last time. When I came back to the convent for supper, the bishop said to me, 'We had a little Miletus scene here about half past five.' (Miletus was the place where St Paul's Christians parted from him showing signs of great sorrow and affection. It is described in the Acts of the Apostles). Many of the faithful Nancheng Catholics, had come to pay their last farewell to the bishop whom they loved very much before his impending expulsion. The Catholics had very kindly sent us in some meat for what they thought would be our last supper together and they also sent us a bottle of rice wine. We drank to the Chinese priests and the bishop's toast was, 'The Chinese Martyrs. The Pope.' We felt very sad at the prospect of leaving those excellent Chinese priests and seminarians, leaving them in their hour of need. Because as they always said, 'Though the Reds may hate the foreigner, they still have a well concealed respect for him; for us Chinese Catholics who do not conform to Red ideals, they have only contempt.'

When I opened the Cathedral about seven o'clock the next morning, Mrs Fu was waiting outside. She began to cry pitifully and said that the worst we could suffer would be expulsion but they, the poor Chinese priests and Catholics, would have to 'eat bitterness' in the years to come. After Mass, Jim Yang, John Chang, Seamus and I each said a few words of encouragement and farewell to the distressed congregation and I shall never forget how pitifully Mrs Fu and her companions cried.

At about half past ten, the headmaster came to take us to our trial. He walked some yards ahead of us and Seamus conversed with him all the way as he feared the headmaster might fall into despair. The careerists who accompanied us shouted at the onlookers and bystanders to come to the trial. Most of the orphans and the old ladies in the compound tearfully asked the bishop to give them his blessing as he passed by.

The trial was to be held in the middle school, a quarter of a mile away from where we lived, and the place was thronged with middle school students and with the ordinary citizens. We were taken into the assembly hall which was packed. We were made to stand with our backs to the stage looking out on the assembly. In the crowd, we could see some pockets of Catholics who smiled to us and waved. At the back of the hall, the long grey beard of the local Protestant Minister was conspicuous. In the front seat, wearing a raincoat and carrying a camera, was the chief of police. On the stage behind us were our accusers. They consisted of the headmaster and nearly all the hospital staff and a number of weak Catholics whom the headmaster had persuaded to join the accusers. In all, there were about twenty. It was a long rectangular hall and there must have been four or five hundred present. From the back wall, Chairman Mao looked down benignly from his coloured print; he was flanked by the late Joseph V. Stalin. On the side walls, the rest of the Red Hierarchy of the day like Anna Pawka, Harry Pollitt and

Togliatti, from similar coloured prints looked approvingly on the assembly. There was a little star-shaped window in red and blue coloured glass at the apex of the wall, just above Mao's and Stalin's pictures.

The headmaster opened the proceedings in his best declamatory manner. He said that he was still a Catholic but that he was a patriot too. Recently, his eyes had been opened and he had seen the light. The excommunication which the bishop levelled at him brought home to him, and his henchmen, the need for reform in the Catholic Church in Nancheng. Then he went on to enumerate the bishop's 'crimes' and the 'crimes' of all the priests who had been in the area for the past twenty years. He dealt at length with Mick Moran's and Jim Yang's crimes. He recalled with bitter sarcasm that Jim Yang in condemning the Patriotic Church had brought the people to tears, and ominously reminded him that there might be a need for tears in the future. Then he listed the 'crimes' of us other priests who were present. As he called out a 'crime' the children would point their fingers at us and quite a lot of the grown-ups would do the same. They hissed slogans like 'Down with the Imperialists'. The headmaster's speech received tumultuous applause, especially the peroration wherein he called for fitting punishment for the criminals. The next accuser was an artist who in a burst of patriotism had abandoned his art and went to study agriculture and work in the fields. The bishop had educated him and now he was making the charge that the bishop had not given him the full education which he deserved.

After him came Lorenzo. At least it sounded like his voice but – could it possibly be Lorenzo? It was his furniture which I had stored in Kiutu church and that action was imputed to me as a crime. It was his father whom Barney O'Neill had bailed out on Christmas Day. When the father, according to the Reds, committed suicide, though we did not believe that, Barney was held responsible and severely punished and, as well as that, we had to pay a fine. Yes – it was the same Lorenzo who had been educated by the Church and afterwards employed by the same institution. Now he had turned against us with a venom which astounded everybody. We heard afterwards that even the Reds were flabbergasted. Of course, fear to some extent drove him to this extreme. He hoped that by posing as an anti-foreigner and anti-imperialist, he might

be spared the fate which generally befell a man who was a landlord's heir.

The bishop and I looked over our shoulders to see Lorenzo de-
claiming but the artist-turned-farmer put a hand on each of our
heads and pushed them downwards shouting 'Shong lin min di
tao', 'Keep your heads bowed in the presence of the people.' He did
the same with Seamus. They expected us to bow our head when
our crimes were mentioned as an acknowledgement of our guilt.

Our accusers were using an oratorical device which I had never
seen before. At the end of each new sentence, they paused and said,
'Oh - oh - oh.' It began like an exclamation and went a little higher
on each 'oh' and then ended like a moan. Lorenzo said, amongst
other interesting things, that the Church had always been on the
side of the landlords and imperialists but now that day was gone –
thanks to the People's Army of Liberation.

For about two hours, the accusations went on and soon they
became very monotonous. The 'leit-motiv' running through the
accusations was largely rice. Some of them had been promised rice
but did not get it, or only got poor quality rice; others had allegedly
been defrauded of rice. In fact, I came to the conclusion that the
bishop must be a 'Rice Criminal'. Rice rather than doctrine was the
issue.

Amongst the accusers was just one man who showed a little
humour. He was, he told us, now a policeman in Nancheng City,
but that he had not always been law-abiding. In fact, in his unre-
generate days, he told us, he had stolen a cow from the Church and
was sent to jail by the authorities but Fr Ellis had bailed him out.
Shortly afterwards, he seemed to fall back into his old habit of cow-
snatching and told us, suiting the action to the word, how Fr Ellis
had called him up when he heard of his relapse into crime. 'Come
here, Peter', said Father Ellis (because the accuser explained to the
audience, he was called Peter in the Catholic Church). When Peter
obeyed, Tom Ellis lifted his hand as to give him a resounding slap.
He demonstrated the dimensions of the threatened slap with ample
gesture and won the hearts of everybody judging by the groans of
applause and sympathy which greeted his remarks. He had also
been maltreated, he claimed, by the Columban Sisters when he was
a patient in the hospital.

The bishop smiled genially to some of the children and pointed back at them when they pointed at him. But some of the Middle School students got catapults and started to lob small stones at us. I found this kind of assault most disconcerting because it is very difficult to look down your nose with dignified hauteur at your scoffers when two or three catapults are being sighted on your glasses. Some of the smaller children started pelting stones at us and the stones were not that small. Their activities were directed by some women of the Patriotic Church Movement.I remember one boy about ten, firing a big stone, almost as big as your fist, right at the bishop. Fortunately, I was able to intercept it before it reached its target. The middle-aged woman director, when she saw the praiseworthy efforts of the young patriot chided him, 75% admiringly, 25% reprovingly and gave him a little slap so that we could see her; then she said to him. 'What do you mean by firing such a big stone at the imperialists?'

Our accusers, almost without exception, had been helped in some notable way by the Church. One of the lady nurses was perhaps our most virulent accuser. She stamped with rage. Two years earlier, when her husband had died she was in dire poverty.The priests of the Cathedral had taken pity on her and brought her into the church compound. There she was trained as a nurse and her two children supported. Eaten rice is soon forgotten.

When the accusations had gone for three and a half hours, Seamus and I were a bit concerned about the bishop because he was now sixty-five. But he stood up to the ordeal with great fortitude and aplomb. After the accusations, we were paraded through Nancheng streets on our way to the court. On the billboards in the city the country people, who had been brought into Nancheng for the trial, could read about our crimes and see the cartoons. On the billboards, they could also read the text of a telegram from two Irish communists wishing their Red brethren in Nancheng good luck in their efforts to bring us Irish imperialists to justice. The communists had brought in thousands of people from all over the county to see foreigners being paraded through the streets – a most unusual and sensational spectacle.

The journey to the court took us through most of the town and I cannot remember how long it lasted but I would say at least an

hour. As we passed along the crowded streets we were jeered at,
spat upon, beaten and kicked. The kicks were benign. The local
people did not 'put the boot in' because they wore cloth shoes with
paper uppers. The local people judge an institution by the amount
of face it possesses. To them, the Church died that day in Nancheng. Every kick was a loss of face – was a nail in its coffin, so to
speak.

In preparation for 'Operation spit' a communal throat clearing took
place in which many seemed to participate. I was not a bit impressed by the citizens who just ran up to us and spat at us from
close range. Admittedly, when one of them landed a spit on your
nose you lost face and this gave a laugh to the bystanders. But I fear
I was a bit impressed by the citizens who stood right where they
were, just cleared their throats and landed their spits with unerring
aim on target. The long-distance spitters showed a certain amount
of flair and panache, and livened up a bit for me what was a dull
parade.

The court-room was a small room with white-washed walls in the
Commissar's compound. In the centre of the room was a desk. Behind it sat two youthful judges, one of them tall and ruddy faced
for a Chinese, the other squat with lifeless eyes. We were not all
that surprised to find that they knew next to nothing about the case
on which they were to pass judgement. The first judge told the
bishop that for the future he was not to go to the countryside to
preach. In fact, no priest had been going to the countryside for a
couple of years. Then the judge warned the bishop that we were
not to make our Confessions for the future and he meant, of course,
that we were not to hear Confessions. Then the other judge requested
the bishop to sign a guarantee that we would obey the law from
now on. The bishop told them that if this meant we should abstain
from renouncing the Patriotic Church Movement then he would
not give any such guarantee. As a Catholic bishop, he said, it was
his duty to point out errors and to denounce them. That he would
continue to do whilst he was bishop. Thereupon they suggested
that the foreign priests could continue hearing Confessions provided that they did not obstruct or sabotage the Patriotic Church
Movement by so doing. This again the bishop refused to guarantee,
saying he would not recognise the right of communists to legislate
on Church affairs. When he had finished his statement, the bishop

turned as he wiped his forehead and said, 'Am I doing alright, boys?' All of us priests replied, 'Very fine.'

Bishop Cleary, Seamus and I and Paul Yu were then returned home under escort and were kept under guard by members of the Patriotic Church Movement. The other two Chinese priests, Jim Yang and John Chang were sent to civilian jail. They were still in the courtroom when we were taken out. About a quarter of a mile from the court, we turned into a side street and as we did so we heard two voices from behind calling, 'Bishop! bishop!' Turning round we saw Jim Yang and John Chang under heavy escort being led off to the civilian jail. They were two outstanding priests and had given magnificent service to the Church since the Reds came to Nancheng and they had been most loyal although they knew very well that such loyalty would brand them as 'running dogs for the imperialists' and could only lead them to years in jail, if not to death. That night we received a note from them asking us to send them bedding and some toilet articles. That was the last we heard of them for some time.

The headmaster was so enraged at Jim Yang that he made no secret of the fact that he would do his utmost to secure the death penalty for him. Some of the Catholics were also fearful about what John Chang's fate might be. He was the spiritual Director of the Legion of Mary and he had chronic tuberculosis and they feared that the hardship of jail would be too much for him, and that he would not live long. We still had one Chinese priest with us, Paul Yu. He belonged to a neighbouring diocese and the Patriotic Church Movement did not trump up any charges against him in Nancheng. They hoped to be able to coax him to join the Movement but he beat them at their own game.

The Sunday after the trial they expected he would say Mass in the Cathedral and hear the Confessions of all who had become members of the Patriotic Church Movement. He was stricken with a very severe diplomatic illness, however, when the headmaster came to call on him at eight o'clock that Sunday morning. So convincing was he in his illness, that the headmaster was full of sympathy. He refused to go to the Cathedral to say Mass for them the next Sunday also. Instead he said Mass in one of the seminarians rooms and about five or six of the faithful Catholics came along.

The day after the trial the bishop, Seamus and I said Mass secretly in the house at different times although we were being watched by our guards. The seminarians were allowed to talk to us. However, we felt that it would be only a matter of days before our expulsion and the seminarians were of the same opinion. They said that the Commissar lacked the necessary permission to expel us and he was waiting for the Provincial Governor to authorise him. The faithful Catholics were very frightened by the fact that two Chinese priests had been sent to jail and that the bishop and foreign priests had been so humiliated. They were afraid to come near the compound because they knew that if they did their names would be noted by the headmaster who would report them to the police.

That afternoon, we had one Catholic visitor who ran the gauntlet. He ignored the headmaster as he passed him, entered our house unannounced and unchallenged by the guards and the first I knew of his presence was when the bishop said to me, 'Your carrier is looking for you upstairs.' It was Shong Yung, who had come in all the way from Kiutu to see us and to sympathise with us on our trial and on the loss of the Chinese priests. As well as being my carrier, he was also a mystic and something of a prophet on the side and a friend.

On February 14th, Seamus and I were washing up after breakfast when a knock came to the kitchen door. The seminarian Peter Hsieh informed me that the Deputy Chief of Police and the head-master were waiting for me outside. I immediately thought of jail and was undecided whether I should go upstairs for my tooth-brush or go out to meet them first. I decided on the latter course. To my surprise and consternation, however, the Deputy Chief of Police gave a big schoolboy grin when he saw me and said, 'How is Comrade Tien? Have you eaten rice to repletion?' I told him that in these days we could not afford rice as they would not allow our money to come in from Hong Kong but that I had partaken of water rice gruel. The Deputy laughed and the headmaster, smiling at me, said, 'Comrade Tien is a very hard worker.' Then we got down to business. The school-boy grin on the Deputy's face gave way to an official threatening stare. 'Comrade Tien,' he said,'you will leave this country at once.'

I was flabbergasted at this unexpected turn of events and the headmaster went on to explain. 'You can prepare now,' he said, 'and leave Nancheng as soon as possible. Of course you have to go to the police office and make final travelling arrangements before your departure.' With that he left.

That afternoon I went to the police office and I was under the impression that I was being expelled. At the office, however, I learned that the visa for which the bishop had applied nearly a year earlier was now granted. The only difficulty was that we had no money. I told them we were in financial straits and asked them if they would release the money which they had taken from us before the trial. They promised to look into the matter.

That same day the artist-turned-farmer, who starred at our trial, had summoned the bishop to the court and claimed that the bishop owed him twenty tan of rice. While I was at the police office the bishop and Seamus were at the court. Jim Yang was allowed out of jail to give evidence. His face was drawn and he looked very worried. During the next few months the bishop was summoned before the court two or three times and eventually compensation was granted to the artist-turned-farmer. The bishop refused to pay so they used the money they had taken from us before the trial. But the artist-turned-farmer did not get it. It went into funds of the Patriotic Church Movement.

During these months, I was getting very tired of being called down to the police office. A small posse of Reds would sometimes come to summon me and I felt like the bad guy in a Western film. The chief of police who had often interrogated me was a man in his mid-twenties, frail in stature, keen eyes and a highly intelligent face. This particular day he was in a vicious mood. I told him, as I had told them in the past, that I would not leave China until they gave me the money which they had taken. I pointed out that our representative in Hong Kong would not send us any more money seeing that the Reds had confiscated the money that had been sent. The chief of police was angry and he said in a loud voice, 'What are you going to do, then? Are you going to stay here? If you do not get money in you cannot eat here. What is going to happen then?'

The bishop had anticipated such a question and he had discussed it with me and I was prepared for it. 'We may die with the hunger, but are glad to die,' I told him, 'with God's help, if that is what God wants. We know that the more we suffer the better things will be for the local Church ultimately. In some mysterious way our sufferings united to Christ's, have power to save and sanctify. The greater our hardships the more quickly those Catholics who have fallen away will return to the fold and recognise again the Pope as Christ's vicar on earth.' Still, I promised that if they released the money which they had confiscated, I would leave the country.

In the meantime, a month had elapsed since the trial and there was no indication that we would soon be expelled so the bishop decided that we would start teaching the seminarians again. He did most of it but Seamus and I helped him. Joe Peng had almost finished his theology and the bishop planned to ordain him as soon as possible. As things were developing, it seemed to me that I should stay on unless I was expelled and the bishop felt that this was the best thing to do.

The communists did not agree with the bishop in this matter. Two or three days after I made the decision, a soldier and a blue-coated official called for me and took me to the police station at about six o'clock in the evening. First I was brought before a security official. 'Why have you not left the country?' he said. His eyes narrowed as he looked at me half curiously, half menacingly. I replied, 'I shall not leave the country until I am expelled.' 'The last time you said you would leave as soon as you got the money. Now you will not leave unless you are expelled. What do you mean by this?' he said, 'You are just trying to deceive the communists,' he added. I explained to him as best I could about how the changing situation had altered my plans. He argued with me for some time and then told me I could return to the church.

I was no sooner back at the church than another soldier and another blue-coat summoned me a second time. It was now seven o'clock. This time I was brought before the chief of police. He sat down behind the old desk which had belonged to the seminary but had been 'borrowed' by the Reds, while I stood in a draught between two open windows. It was a piercing cold night in February.

He struck the table and harangued me for about ten minutes. Joseph Peng, the seminarian, accompanied me as I needed someone to interpret the northern dialect, especially when they talked fast. He accompanied me, too, for another reason. The bishop felt that I should have someone with me in case the communists detained me during their interrogation. The chief of police said I was just blackguarding the Reds; one day I said I would go if I had the money, the next day I said I would not go unless I was expelled. The Red Regime was not going to stand for any such impudence from foreigners. By this time he was shouting at the top of his voice.

In his excitement the chief of police not only shouted but also spoke much faster than he had spoken at the beginning. Again he banged his fist on the table and seemed to pick up more speed as he proceeded with his diatribe. I said to Joseph Peng, 'What is he saying?' 'Oh, he's saying very obscene things,' answered Joe. The chief continued for about five minutes more and I asked Joe 'What's he saying now?' 'Oh terribly filthy things,' replied Joseph and a look of pain enveloped his countenance. After a while the chief lowered his voice and said, 'If it is not blackguarding, why are you changing your mind?' I then explained that the bishop was an old man and that there was only one other foreign priest, Seamus, with him and if one of them got sick, it would place the other in a very difficult position.

'The three of you intend to stay here?' he said. 'Yes,' I replied, 'We intend to stay until we are expelled. Our place is here with the Catholics.' 'Well,' he said, 'the sufferings of Christ might do some good but I cannot see what good the hardships you are suffering will do to anybody.' To this most unexpected response, I made no reply partly because I feared he was mocking. However, he lapsed into silence and after a few minutes he asked Joseph Peng a few questions about whether he still prayed and about the number who came to prayers and to Mass.

After Joseph replied the chief of police lapsed again into silence for a few more minutes and then said, as if he were talking to himself, 'I am a Catholic.' The effect of this statement on us was just overwhelming. Not since Air Vice-Marshal Brown, on board the Empress of Australia, had offered us a case of Scotch out of the blue, was I so badly stuck for words. You could have knocked us over with a wren's feather. 'I mean,' he continued, 'I was a Catholic. I was educated in Catholic schools but I am now more progressive.'

I felt remorseful because I had raised my voice at him earlier in the argument. Actually he had shouted at me for about five minutes first, and I suppose when you are living under heavy tension and fear shout borrows shout. I felt great sympathy for the man, too, and strange to say, I felt very close to him and I think he felt close to Joseph Peng and myself. 'Whether you have become progressive or not,' I reminded him, 'you still have the faith and you still have a soul, and you have to work for your salvation. You are running great danger of losing your faith.' He did not take any offence at my remarks; in fact, he said with a shrug of the shoulders, 'You know my father and mother still say their prayers,' 'I suppose,' said I, 'that they are praying that you will come back to the Church. I shall continue to pray for the same intention.'

Then he stood up and motioned to us that the interview was at an end. As it had lasted practically three hours, Joseph Peng and I were tired from standing and perished with the cold. On my way back, I thought of things I should have said which might have helped the poor man. My hindsight was always at its most brilliant immediately after I had suffered a severe brow-beating from the People's Army of Liberation.

A month after the trial, the headmaster returned the key of the convent church to Paul Yu. He gave Paul Yu permission to hold church services there. During the Sundays previous to that, a handful of Catholics had been coming to Mass in the seminarians' room. There was no doubt about it, however, that the trial and its aftermath had a paralysing effect even on the faithful Catholics. I remember meeting one or two former catechists who had joined the Patriotic Church. A couple of years earlier they had been influential people in Nancheng parish; now they passed us by as if they never had known us.

A few weeks later, the headmaster told us that he intended to convert the convent building where we lived into hospital wards and for that reason he would have to evict us from the convent. Our new abode, he said, was to be the wash-house, a squat one-storey building with two rooms. The bishop, hearing of the plan, wrote to the chief of police and the latter sent back the letter to the bishop, but in a few days came to visit us. He was accompanied by the headmaster and both exuded charm and good fellowship. I had met them downstairs and they asked to be taken to see the bishop.

The four of us sat in the bishop's room and talked. The headmaster promised that he would get the money which he had confiscated from us before the trial. We told him that our fare was the poorest, that we had only an ounce or two of meat a week for four of us, that we lacked summer clothing as we had given our clothing away. The police chief admitted that the bishop was an old man and that all this was very hard on him. 'There is, however,' he added, 'an alternative which would be easier for you. 'The alternative, of course, was to leave China.

The bishop affirmed that we would not leave until we were expelled. He appealed to both of them to allow him some money, if not for our maintenance, at least for the maintenance of the few orphans who still depended on us. They promised they would do this and then left, taking leave of us in a very courteous and deferential manner.

We often felt, during the early part of that year, that the attitude of the Reds towards us depended on how things were going in Korea. If the news was favourable for them they were polite, if it was unfavourable they were overbearing and offensive. Looking back from the distance of a year, we could easily see how the overthrow of the Church in Nancheng diocese was hastened by the unexpected Chinese successes of December 1950 in Korea. Indeed, Mike Halford had told me away back that the overthrow of the Church in southern China was put forward by three years as a result of these heady but temporary victories in Korea.

Around this time, some of the Red officials went out of their way to be polite to us for another reason. A purge was being carried out inside the communist Party itself. The chief objective of this purge was to root out corruption. In the course of the purge, many pillars of the movement were liquidated. The Nancheng Reds had 'borrowed' lots of furniture from the church, borrowed it in the name of the Party but some of the officials had used that furniture for their own private use.

The anti-corruption campaign aimed not only at combating corruption, waste and bureaucracy, but also had as an objective the recovery of stolen property for the Red administration. In Nancheng the head tax officer had already been imprisoned on charges of using tax money for his own private budget.

Day by day, we were expecting to be evicted from the convent. Then there were rumours that the jail, not the wash-house, would be our destination.

On one such day, I was walking with the bishop in front of the convent, when suddenly he said, his blue eyes twinkling with merriment, 'I wonder shall I live up to my principles if and when we are put in jail?' 'What principles?' I asked. 'Of course,' he retorted with a laugh, 'you think that bishops have no principles at all.' I told him that I wouldn't go quite that far and asked him what principles he had in mind. 'Hunger strike,' he said, laughing with amusement. His mention of hunger-strike was a reference to a controversy into which he was drawn thirty-two years earlier. In 1920, Terence McSwiney, the Lord Mayor of Cork, had been imprisoned by the British and had gone on hunger strike as a protest and against British policy in Ireland. After seventy days Terence McSwiney died of hunger. Some theologians maintained that his action was unethical, that it was suicide. Doctor Cleary, as he then was, defended the hunger strike in a few able articles in theological magazine. He did this, I understand, well before Terence McSwiney died. It was a legitimate protest by McSwiney, against the British oppression of the time. 'Well,' said I to the bishop, 'if you take my advice you won't follow your principles. You should eat whatever you get because it is a starvation diet anyhow.' He told me he defended hunger strike as a protest, but not to death. Actually, the bishop told me afterwards that he had left Maynooth and joined the Maynooth Mission to China, as the Columbans were called in the early days, when he was drawn into this controversy. He said that his friend, Jerry Kinnane, then a professor on the Maynooth staff (afterwards Archbishop of Cashel), asked Dr Cleary to reply to a theologian from Clonliffe College, which he did.

CHAPTER 18

The Agony of Paul Lee

There was little communication between Nancheng and the southern part of the diocese in the spring of 1951. But early in May, a Catholic from Nanfeng called at the church. The Catholics there, it seemed, were loyal to their faith and persevering in prayer. They did not suffer the ordeal of the Patriotic Church Movement in all its fury as the Nancheng Catholics had. One of the most horrific items of news brought by the Catholic was, to my mind, the story (and manner) of Paul Lee's death. Other Nanfeng Catholics who called corroborated the story.

A little background is necessary, so we shall flash back to that sunny mellow October day in 1950 when I was visiting Mike Halford in Kaopi. The latter was very busy in his dispensary, so he told his catechist, Paul, and his house-boy, Hen Chi Ho, to entertain me. I sat with them in the common room in the teacher's house and Paul was very entertaining. He was a small stoutish man of about sixty or so. His face was dour and stern in repose but when he smiled it became suffused with warmth and friendliness. He gave the position on his life and times and was very interesting to listen to because his life story embraced, or impinged on, the history of the local Church for the past half century.

As a boy of ten he had known something of the Boxer rising in Jiangsi. He had seen the last days of the crumbling Manchu dynasty and the rise of the Republic in 1911. As a catechist, he had worked for the French Vincentian Fathers. When the first Columbans came to the Nancheng district in 1927, led by Cornie Tierney, Paul was one of the first old Catholics to meet them. He had been in Nanfeng when Tim Leonard was murdered by the Reds in 1929. He knew Monsignor Quinlan, later Archbishop Quinlan of Korea, and worked with him when the latter was trying to negotiate Cornie Tierney's release. For years he had been a catechist for Pat Dermody,

Mick Moran, Gerry Buttimer and, after his arrest, Mike Halford. In later years, he had been living in Lienchu, where he had some rice fields and was classed as a landlord.

When things were getting hot in Lienchu, six months before, he had 'baled out' and had eventually arrived in Kaopi. Recently he had been installed as catechist in one of Mike Halford's country missions. The Lienchu people were unaware of his Kaopi habitat.

That morning, he was in a hilarious mood as he told one funny story after another. He was rather hard of hearing but that defect did not bother him much as he never was the type who would have made a good listener anyhow. Yet, as I listened to him, I could not help reflecting that there was something artificial about his hilarity. Something like the forced hilarity of the schoolboy who has escaped a 'hiding' but who is apprehensive that a hiding might be in the offing any time. I sensed an air of fatalism like soft background music behind the joviality. Hen Chi Ho had been a junior seminarian and only recently had returned from the Junior Seminary at Zikawei, Shanghai. In Shanghai he had seen many of the Russian advisers, who had come to help Red China. He asserted that the Russians looked down on the Chinese and treated them with contempt. They even treated high-ranking Chinese officers like dirt. Paul and Mr Hen had become fast friends. Hen Chi Ho was a native of Lienchu and had known Paul there.

Mike Halford was arrested at Christmas 1950, and early in February was in Nancheng. The Church in Kaopi was closed down. Two weeks later Hen Chi Ho arrived in Nancheng on his way home. He was deeply depressed at the closing down of the Kaopi church and his hatred of the Reds seemed to be burning with even a brighter flame than it had three months earlier. He informed me that his mother had a bit of land in Lienchu and he intended to go back to the land and work on it, hoping thereby to escape communist influence. The Reds were now seeking to brain-wash the youths of the county. He had hoped that by becoming a farmer the Reds would regard his brain as not worth washing. Then he left us. A month later we were surprised to hear that Hen Chi Ho had joined a Communist Cadet School in Foochow.

One bright morning in May 1951, I was having my breakfast after saying Mass in the convent, when who came in but Paul Lee. He looked tired and depressed. Said he, 'The Militia from Lienchu have come for me. They are waiting for me outside now. They allowed me to come in here for a few minutes. Would you please hear my confession and anoint me as I am sure this is the end for me

'Well, Paul,' said I, 'you have walked forty miles in the past couple of days, you plan to walk forty more to Lienchu. You are not a fit subject for Extreme Unction, as the Anointing of the sick was then called, but I shall hear your confession and give you Communion.' I followed the pastoral practice of that day and age. He received Holy Communion with great fervour and said to me, 'Please give me a plenary indulgence in danger of death.' 'Paul,' I said, 'not all the landlords are killed. You have never defrauded people.' 'Ah,' he said, 'I know, but I feel that I am going to my death.' I cannot remember exactly whether or not he told me that it was his erstwhile friend, Hen Chi Ho who had reported his whereabouts to the Lienchu Reds. If Paul did not tell me that, someone else did. I could not believe it and discounted it as a rumour. A seminarian could not do that, I thought. Paul left the church and continued sorrowfully on his way.

Two months later, Hen Chi Ho returned from his communist training course. He was all 'sharpened up' and dressed in a blue uniform. He swaggered around the compound and carried his revolver where everybody could see it. He called on the seminarians and asked them officiously, 'Is the foreigner still allowed to have church services here?' When he was informed that such was the case, he said it was incredible and took a mental note of the irregularity, as if he were going to check up with a higher authority. He then gave the usual story about his eyes having been opened, etc., and finished up by asking a Chinese priest to say Mass for his mother who had recently died. With a click of his heels he strutted out of the room and returned to Lienchu. He did not call on me as he did the last time.

Two months after that, I heard Paul, his wife, his son and his son's wife had been tortured in turn, tied up and given a 'ride in an airplane'. 'A ride in an airplane' (Tso Hui Gee) means that they were hung by the thumbs from the roof of their own house and beaten senseless. Then a bucket of cold water was thrown over them and they revived. After that, they were made to kneel on broken glass and subjected to indignities. An interval of rest would then be given them and then another 'airplane ride' followed by beatings etc. This went on from morning till night. The 'ride' had lasted for three or four hours. The Red official who presided and made the arrangements for the 'ride' was none other than Hen Chi Ho. He denounced Paul in the most abusive language and told him to give up the gold which he had received from the Church. After the 'ride', they were placed under house arrest. Two or three soldiers guarded them night and day. Week after week the 'rides' continued. In October or November, Hen Chi Ho decided to make an all-out effort to break Paul. For six hours, Paul and his son and the two women were 'hoisted up' naked. They were beaten continuously by Hen Chi Ho and his henchmen. Finally, mentally and physically worn out, Paul consented to give sixty tan of rice, if they released them. It was about midnight when they were cut down from the horizontal beams from which they had been suspended.

Paul asked for three days in which to get the rice. The Reds agreed. The soldiers then led them back to their house. It was now around one o'clock. The soldiers stayed with them for some time but when they noticed that they had now begun to pray they went outside and stood guard at the doors. Paul and his family had obtained some scanty clothing. They kept on praying loudly. While they were in the midst of their prayers, Paul's little grandson, about six or seven, who had been asleep in a neighbouring house, came in. Paul took a bottle of poison and coaxed the little boy to drink it. The little boy tasted it but spat it out when he discovered how bitter it was. The prayers continued on and they rested for a while.

About 3 o'clock they started to pray again. The soldiers came in and saw that they were making the Stations of the Cross. The Chinese sing when they make the Stations and the melody is a haunting one. Each member of the family had a crucifix to which the indulgence for making the Stations was attached. When they had finished the Stations, it was around four o'clock. Paul then solemnly took the bottle of poison, which his grandson had refused, put it to his lips and drank about a couple of spoonfuls of it. His wife, son and daughter-in-law did the same. Still, they kept on praying but now it was getting near dawn and they feared they would not be dead when the soldiers came in to summon them. In desperation, Paul got a long rope and cut it in four pieces, it appears. Anyhow, when the soldiers entered the house at about 5 o'clock they found the four members of the family hanging lifeless from the rafters. The nooses of the ropes were taut around their necks. The crucifixes were held tightly in their hands as they swung to and fro. The crucifix in Paul's hand was held so tightly that it was with great difficulty that the Reds were able to remove it.

CHAPTER 19

Strike the Shepherd

Towards the end of June, 1952, some Catholics from Mike Halford's parish visited us. Two of them were Dee Fee Min and his wife. He was a native of Kiutu and had been a catechist in Kaopi parish. Both of them were outstanding in their loyalty to the church and to Mike Halford during the dark days. The most unexpected bit of sad news they brought us was that George had committed suicide during the anti-corruption movement. He had been accused of being friendly with the landlords and his trial was scheduled for the day after he committed suicide. He simply put the barrel of his Colt 45 revolver into his mouth and blew his head off.

From Mick Moran's parish came word that one of Mick's principal accusers was also running foul of the Red regime. He had been classified as a landlord and he planned to flee from his home town but he was pursued and captured by the Reds. The news from Luki, Pat Sheehy's parish was that the Catholics had been threatened that unless they gave up their holy pictures and Rosary beads and other religious objects they would not receive any land. Some of the weaker Catholics, fearing that such threats would be implemented, proceeded to hand in the sacred objects. This was regarded as a sign of apostasy by the Commissar. However, when the land was eventually divided, no distinction was made between those who handed in their religious articles and those who had not.

When the anti-corruption campaign was finished in Nancheng, other campaigns were started because the Reds believed in keeping the people in a state of tension all the time. There was even an anti-pest campaign. Each citizen was expected to catch and destroy a certain quota of flies during the summer. Then there was a 'comfort for the troops' campaign. The comforts which were sent from our part of the country to the Chinese soldiers in Korea were mostly turnips. We also had an 'anti-idea' campaign. It was an attempt to win the minds of the youth and it was carried out by showing up the alleged silliness of ideas other than those approved of by the Red regime.

Earlier they had combatted the Buddhist and Taoist doctrines but strange to say they permitted the practice of these religions once again. They feared that in suppressing them they would be only courting more unpopularity and they felt that they were unpopular enough.

In July, the Bishop ordained Joseph Peng to the Sub-deaconate. A month later he was a deacon and then on August 6th, the Feast of the Transfiguration, he was ordained to the priesthood. The headmaster was indignant and angry and did his best to have the police stop the ordination but they refused to be implicated in the affair. Without their active help he was powerless.

In preparation for the ordination, Seamus and I gave a six day retreat to Joseph Peng and to the three junior seminarians, Tommy Yu, Peter Hsieh and Joseph Yu. The junior seminarians had requested the Bishop to give them Minor orders and he did so a couple of weeks later.

The account of the ordination, written by Seamus in Columban Mission in 1982 is much better than mine. Here it is and I quote:

'I have participated in papal ceremonies in Rome, notably the funeral Masses for Pope Paul VI and the installation Mass of Pope John Paul I. But no papal Masses nor pontifical ceremonies anywhere will live in my memory as vividly as that ordination in Communist China in which I participated.

It was stark in its simplicity. It took place in a small room. The altar was an office desk, the Bishop's throne was a swivel chair and when Joe prostrated himself before the altar, his feet touched the opposite wall. At one stage of the ceremony the Bishop was apprehensive lest we step over Joe as he lay prostrate on the floor. But the presence and the power of the Holy Spirit were very evident there that morning. After ordination and a simple breakfast, Joe went about his chores. I can still see him trotting off with a bucketful of scraps to feed the pig we were fattening for eventual sale'.

Joseph Peng had come through a very hard school during the past couple of years but had come through with very high honours.

With remarkable daring, he attacked the headmaster more than once and I had noted his gallantry on Christmas morning. Before him, as far as one could see, lay nothing except hardships and trials and jail, and probably early death. Life as a deacon would have been easier for him yet he told the Bishop that he dearly wished to be ordained a priest at this time although he knew that ordination would immediately make him a marked man. Three of the four Chinese priests of the diocese were already in jail. As I watched the newly-ordained priest giving his blessing to the Bishop and to the Catholics, I could not help reflecting that the Church in Nancheng was not dead yet. Father Peng's leadership would be an inspiration to the Catholics and a challenge to the Reds. It was a landmark in Catholic resistance in Nancheng city and diocese.

After Joe Peng's ordination, and probably as a result of it, the Mass attendance increased. This increase was galling to the headmaster and his helpers so they enlisted the aid of the middle school students as a counterblast. Each Sunday morning, twenty or thirty of the middle school students would enter the convent church and stare at the Catholics in an angry fashion hoping to demoralise them without having recourse to physical interference. When the students noticed that some Catholics were stealthily entering the convent to go to confession, they followed them, and when they noticed the Bishop saying Mass in an inner room, they began to shout and jeer at the top of their voices. The Catholics who were participating in the bishop's Mass, or were making their confessions in the rooms where Seamus and I were hearing, instantly became frightened and left the convent at once.

Soon it became necessary for us to lock the doors of the convent when the middle school students were around. We still managed to hear some confessions as the Catholics could enter the convent through a passageway from the church. Soon, however, the students discovered the passageway and followed them. Whenever the students saw a foreigner even saying Mass or hearing confessions, they would begin to shout and frighten the people and obstruct the ceremony.

Then we had to bar the door between the oratory and the convent but even when all the doors were barred, the students still managed to come in. Sometimes they would look in the windows and tap on them and shout 'Down with the Imperialists'. But other times they would pound loudly on the doors and demand admittance under threat of breaking down the doors. Sunday mornings became rather hectic times for us but still we managed to hear a number of confessions in spite of the obstruction.

The seminarians, of course, were of great assistance to us. One of them would watch out the window while we were hearing confessions and as soon as he saw the middle school students approaching, he would lock the door. Then when the attention of the students was diverted he would unlock the door and let in more Catholics who wanted to go to confession.

To our great delight, we had a record attendance on the Feast of the Assumption, 1952. There were about seventy people from Kiutu and Catholics from Vincent McNally's, Mick Moran's and Seamus O'Reilly's parishes also attended. All were greatly encouraged at the sight of Father Joe Peng saying Mass. The Kiutu Catholics, ever since my expulsion, and especially since my trial on the 8th February, had been coming in on weekdays for confession and Communion. I do not recall the exact number who came in on weekdays but I imagine it went into the hundreds. While I was in Nancheng, sometimes they would bring us eggs, sometimes a few pounds of meat.

In October, the headmaster informed Paul Yu that a big meeting was to be held in Nanchang, the capital of the Province. Chinese priests were requested by the Government to attend and the object of the meeting was to try to get all Chinese priests to join the Patriotic Church Movement. Unfortunately, in the capital, two Chinese priests had already joined. They had ganged-up against Archbishop Chou, the Archbishop of Nanchang, and had falsely accused him of collaborating with the Japanese during the Sino-Japanese War.

Paul Yu refused to go. Again, he did not act in a defiant way, but very effectively. He thwarted the plans of the Patriotic Church establishment using the same tactics as on a former occasion. Again he was stricken with a critical diplomatic illness accompanied by frightening symptoms of moans and groans.

Then one morning, at about 7.30, a few days before the Feast of Christ the King, that is the last Sunday in October – the Bishop was startled when he saw Fr Jim Yang, accompanied by guards, enter the convent church. The Bishop went to the church immediately and Father Yang accompanied him outside. Father Yang, said that he had been sent by the Prison Director to get a pruning knife so that he could plant some trees in the prison grounds and orange shrubs.

As the guards would not let him out of their sight, he could not go to confession, so one of us gave him absolution. He had a convict's haircut but he looked better than we had seen him the last time. The Bishop regarded the permission given to Jim Yang to visit us as an act of kindness by Mr Sun, the Chief of Police. The Bishop's expulsion was in the offing and Mr Sun, recognising the friendship that existed between Jim Yang and the Bishop, kindly decided to let Jim see the Bishop for the last time. Jim told us that he had seen Luke Teng and John Chang a short time previously and he said that both of them were well.

On St Columban's Day, November 23rd, we were having dinner with the seminarians when Joseph Wu, one of the seminarians, out of the blue, asked the Bishop, 'Monsignor, would it be possible for us to apply to the Shanghai seminary? When you are expelled things will be very difficult for us. If we could get to a seminary and continue our studies – that would be a very satisfactory arrangement'. The idea had not occurred to us.

The Bishop did not think there was much hope as one could not travel to Shanghai without consulting the Reds and getting their permission. It seemed rather unlikely that they would allow seminarians to continue their studies. Still, there was always a chance because we had often noticed that there was not a lot of co-operation between different branches of the Red Administration. In our experience at city and provincial levels, there seemed to be a lack of co-ordination between different Red departments.

Then, to our great surprise and joy, a letter came from Shanghai from Ted MacElroy on the 8th December. He told us that he would be able to get the Nancheng seminarians into the seminary at Shanghai but that the matter would have to be cleared with the local Red authorities. He did not anticipate there would be much difficulty. He would make the arrangements at the Shanghai end and suggested that the boys travel separately. When we got the letter on the Feast of the Immaculate Conception, we knew Our Lady was looking after us.

Meanwhile preparations for our next trial, which was scheduled for Sunday December 14th, were being hastily made. On December 11th, at nine o'clock at night, a messenger from the Commissar's office arrived with a written order. The order was that the insignia of the Legion of Mary should be handed over within twelve hours. The Bishop refused to hand it over and he also refused to acknowledge the Government's right to interfere in religious matters.

The next morning, the Bishop was called down to the court and was mulcted for thirty tan of rice. A tan is the equivalent of fifty-six pounds. A court official said that this amount of rice was compensation for the artist-turned-farmer – who had claimed at his first trial that the Bishop had failed to give him a liberal education. After several hearings of this case, the Bishop appealed to the higher court, and the higher court decided that the original thirty tan of rice should be raised to thirty-six tan. The Bishop refused to pay the fine, and the Red officials confiscated the money which they had held in the bank since our previous trial.

On Sunday morning, 14th December, there was another Miletus scene. The faithful Catholics had come in tears to bid goodbye to their Bishop and to ask for his blessing. The rumour going the rounds that Sunday morning was that the same team of accusers would take the stage as on the previous occasions. The Bishop's one-time houseboy had refused to join the accusers at the first trial and had held out bravely since in spite of repeated threats. We had felt sure that he could not stand firm this time, because really they had lots of things against him. He had been influential with the Nationalist regime, among many other things. Still, we had hoped against hope that he might wriggle out of the dilemma. Our hopes were dashed to the ground, on that Sunday morning, when his wife came into the room when I was hearing confessions and started to cry bitterly. She said, as she wiped her tears away, 'Thanks to the Bishop, thanks to the priests. There is no way out this time'.

After Mass that Sunday, more Catholics came to pay a sorrowful farewell to the Bishop and the priests. The middle school students soon swarmed down on us and there were a couple of hundred of them in all. They entered the house, surrounded the three of us and began to shout 'Imperialists, American spies' and other derogatory slogans. Somehow or other, we managed to eat a bit of lunch but from tiffin time until three o'clock, they did not let us move. The students cornered us in the corridors and kept asking ridiculous questions, poking fun at us, jeering at us and mocking us. They were still tormenting us when the Deputy Chief of Police and a soldier arrived at three o'clock. The Deputy formally read out the summons, addressing the Bishop and then marched him off. We got the surprise of our lives when he told us we were not to accompany the Bishop but that we were to stay at home.

As usual, the Reds had left us guessing and had done the one thing we did not expect. Seamus and I were discussing the various possibilities as to how the situation might develop, when about half past four, two visitors came to see me. One of them was Mi Fung who had been in charge of the orphanage in Kiutu and the other was an excellent Catholic, Di Fee Min's wife, who had helped Mike Halford so effectively. They had attended the Bishop's trial and then very thoughtfully rushed back to give us the news. The Bishop, they said, was compelled to stand on a bench during the trial, soldiers stood on either side with rifles and bayonets at the ready. He had to stand facing the audience with the stage at his back as in the former trial.

The women related that Lorenzo, who had been Comprador in the Nancheng compound, turned particularly malicious while making his charges against the Bishop. He explained to the audience that the Bishop had deceived him. The Bishop's houseboy, too, acted his part with great artistry and finesse. He claimed that he had been oppressed by the Bishop. Pointing his finger at the latter, as he burned with righteous indignation, he sneered 'You old crook, you have tyrannised and lorded it over me for the past twenty years. But now the boot is on the other foot. The wages you paid me were parsimonious'.

As well as being accused of exploiting the Chinese workmen, the Bishop was also charged with having the Legion of Mary in his diocese, of interfering with the Patriotic Church Movement and of giving bad medicine to the poor and of excommunicating the leaders of the Patriotic Church Movement. After each charge was levelled at him, the audience pointed accusing fingers at the Bishop and the cheer-leader asked the people in a loud sing-song voice, 'Should Li Pai Kao be expelled?' As one would expect the answer was always in the affirmative.

Later we heard that the trial had lasted about two and a half hours and that the sentence was read out by the Mandarin from a document which had been prepared long before the trial. The Mandarin was Diu Gen. He had been the local government boss in Kiutu when I was there. He sentenced the Bishop to eternal expulsion from China within twenty-four hours. After sentence was passed, the Bishop was led back to the church under guard. Seamus and I were locked in our rooms and were placed under guard also. Guards paraded the corridor all that night.

After midnight, the Deputy Chief of Police, accompanied by the headmaster and other Red officials, searched the Bishop's rooms and asked him to hand over the standard of the Legion of Mary. This he refused to do and they took the standard away with them. They searched our two rooms also but took away nothing except a few photographs.

The next morning, Seamus and Joe Peng were told they could go to the bank to draw out sufficient money for the Bishop's travelling expenses. I tried a few times to engage in conversation with the Bishop but each time the guards drove me away. About ten o'clock an official from the police office, accompanied by a couple of soldiers, came to take the Bishop to the bus. They allowed me to carry his bags. When we got downstairs, the Bishop said it would be better if they would allow us to leave by the back door and thus we could avoid the centre of the town in our walk to the bus station. The police officer was adamant and said we would have to parade through down-town Nancheng

The policeman led the procession, next came the Bishop, flanked on either side by a Red soldier, then I brought up the rear carrying the Bishop's luggage. The hospital staff who had accused the Bishop stood watching us. They looked uneasy and a little surly. I asked him if he would like to have a last look at the Cathedral. 'We'll try,' he said sorrowfully. But we had ascended only two or three of the steps leading up to the Cathedral when we were pulled back by the soldiers and ordered to march quickly.

As we reached the outer gate, the Bishop turned back and gave a sad and fleeting glance at the compound which had been his home and scene of his labours for over twenty years; then he took out his handkerchief and wiped away the tears from his eyes. He was the first Bishop of Nancheng and it was the height of bitterness for him to see the Communists undo much of the good work he had done.

As we marched down the town, Catholics rushed out from their houses to take a last look at their Bishop and to escort him to the bus station. But time and again, they were driven back. Some of them, however, persevered in their efforts and whenever they were driven back, they just turned down a side street and reappeared at a later stage in the journey. The Bishop was not allowed to speak to me on the way but whenever we came to a hill, and there were two or three of them on the route, the Bishop would slow his pace to make it easier for me, although the baggage was not heavy. The wife of the Bishop's houseboy was one of the Catholics who persevered all the way, as did many others. There was no shouting or jeering but there was much sadness and tears.

Eventually we reached the bus station and Seamus and Joseph Peng were already there with the money. The Bishop was taken to the Customs office, his bags were searched and then he was brought under guard and put on the bus. As the bus pulled out, he waved to us and to the other Catholics and then the police told us to go home. A few guards accompanied the Bishop on his five day journey to the border.

'Strike the shepherd,' writes the prophet Zechariah 'that the sheep may be scattered.' We were not scattered, but despondent, confused.

All the loyal Catholics and the seminarians, and all us priests, were very down-cast after the Bishop's departure. We missed him very much. On the other hand, the Patriotic Church crowd were triumphant and boasted about the way they had engineered the Bishop's trial and expulsion. They were cock-a-hoop. Their morale seemed to be higher than at any other point since the beginning of the Patriotic Church Movement whereas our morale seemed to have reached an all-time low. We were in the 'Slough of Despond'. This was partly due to the fact that once again the Reds had confused us by not expelling Seamus and me when the Bishop was expelled.

In a highly prolific rumour-producing belt like ours, one would have expected a spate of highly imaginative rumours after the Bishop's expulsion. And they came thick and fast. Some said the Bishop was in jail in Nanchang the capital of the province. Others recalled the fate of Fr Theunnisson, and said you could never tell what punishment the Reds would mete out to the Bishop or to Seamus and me, who were mysteriously left behind. The heavy darkness of uncertainty hung over us. No point in trying to read the signs of the times – the visibility was far too poor.

CHAPTER 20

Eleventh Hour Workers

When the bishop saw that Seamus and I were being left behind, he told us to apply for visas after his departure. But he was a very intelligent man and knew that we could depend on the Communists to do the unpredictable while we were in China. For instance, they could allow one of us to leave and not give a visa to the other. To cater for such an eventuality, the bishop told us before he left that he was appointing both of us Vicars General. Having taken this precaution, he felt he could leave the next move to the Communists.

Anyhow, we told the chief of police that the Bishop had asked us to apply for visas and he seemed very relieved and he said that he would have them by the middle of January.

We had a very big crowd for the Masses on Christmas Day. Not only the Nancheng Catholics, but also Catholics from most of the surrounding parishes attended. There were about eighty from Kiutu for that occasion.

The Kiutu Catholics had a lot of things to talk about that Christmas. They told me that those who had apostatised in the beginning of the Land Division now wanted to retract and come back to the church. 'Dead with the Hunger' had gone to his reward but he had not died of hunger as he always feared he would. Wang Gee Poo had been changed to another district to the delight of the Kiutu people. He had been accused during the anti-Corruption Campaign and according to some of them he had been sent to jail. Poor Shay Yung had married a Red official but he never got a day's health and she was very unhappy.

Mr Dong who had accompanied me when I was on the run and who had given yeoman service to the Church all during the persecution, still held on to his faith. In fact, he was outstanding amongst all the teachers of the county. In public meetings and in private, when he was brow-beaten by our Nancheng headmaster, he always told them that on no account would he apostatise even if he lost his job. Not only that, but he came in regularly to the church in Nancheng while I was there for Confession and Holy Communion, passing on his way in the office of the Patriotic Church Movement. His fortitude was really amazing as some of the members of his family had apostatised.

As well as giving me the news, the Kiutu Catholics told me that in their opinion the Bishop's decision was the correct one. They said that Seamus and I should leave China now and that we would be back with God's help in a few years. They pointed to the fact that the Americans were winning in Korea, or had won there, and that their victory boded ill for the Chinese Communists. Parting with them was always painful.

Early in January, Tommy Yu rushed into my room and said 'Thoni's waiting for you outside'. I went out and there was a brand new Thoni, in a new blue uniform, two revolvers dangling from holsters on his belt, a blue peaked cap and about half a dozen fountain pens in his breast pocket. He held out his hand and greeted me warmly in a kind of a northern accent. Then he came into my room and sat down and told me his story.

When he was unable to get into the seminary in Shaown, he was afraid to stay in Kiutu any longer as the local Reds hated him, so he decided to look for a job. The only job available was working for the local Reds and he did not want that. Then he heard that scholarships were available in Linchuan. He won a scholarship and after six months' training in commercial and business matters, he was given a job in the Forestry Department. He was fortunate because all he was expected to do in that Department was his work and there was little Red propaganda and no brain-washing in the Forestry Section. He was appointed to a county town and soon became Assistant to the County boss. The latter liked Thoni very much and never once asked him about his religion. He had worked hard and faithfully for a year and was now second in command in the whole area in which his Department operated. That was an area covering two counties. He looked as boyish and precocious as ever in spite of his responsibility.

He told me he had attended a training course on forestry some months earlier and that a Russian instructor was running the course. The latter had struck the table and said 'You Chinese are a thousand years behind the times. You've got to step on it'. He found all the Russians very arrogant indeed. He also informed me that every week he and his Department had a kind of a 'Chapter of Faults'. Each person had the right and duty to criticise the way the others did their work. However, the rank and file would rarely dare to criticise the big boss, but none of the rest was free from criticism. He felt that this made for efficiency. He admitted that one lived in a state of tension all the time under the Red Regime. He had become quite influential in the Forestry Department and was now planning to get jobs for many of the Kiutu people, especially carpenters and tradesman of one kind or another. Most of his salary he gave to his father and mother. He told me he had been to Confession and Communion secretly in Linchuan on his way to Nancheng.

On the 15th January, we left Nancheng. Many of the Catholics came to pay us a last visit during the preceding days. Shin Faih, the carpenter, Mi Fung, who now said she was going to take up dressmaking in Pakan, and quite a few others came from Kiutu. Shong Yung was rather melancholy and pessimistic. 'I will never see the face of God,' he moaned. 'If you don't, who will?' asked the seminarian Tommy Yu, who was with us. 'You're pretty well a saint already.' 'I am no saint,' retorted Shong Yung, 'I am the devil's head and I am eaten with pride. But how can one become a saint nowadays,' he continued, 'seeing that we have no Mass, no Blessed Sacrament from now on? All our Churches will be taken over'.

We were rather heavy-hearted about leaving, but the fact that we had been preparing to leave so often kind of dulled our sorrow. Many of these people, not only from Nancheng but from other parishes, had brought us presents of meat and eggs before our departure. They had given us a similar treat before the Bishop departed.

Paul Yu and Joseph Peng felt fairly confident that they would be allowed to continue their pastoral ministrations after our departure, and to our great delight the three seminarians had got permission to resume their studies in Shanghai and were to leave in a few days. The three of them, Tommy Yu, Joseph Wu and Peter Hsieh, were overjoyed and looked forward to the day when they would return to Nancheng as ordained priests.

A number of Catholics, including Mrs Fu and Thung Gwa, came to the bus to see us off. As the bus was about to start, Fu Jen, who used to be our cook in the convent, handed me a bag of buns which she had made for our journey. One of the customs officers shouted rather angrily, 'Let me see that bag'. He grabbed the bag from me as the bus pulled out and I never got the buns back. As the bus was leaving, the Catholics were waving to us and we kept looking back until we rounded a corner and could see them no more.

The first night we spent in a Fan Tien – a Chinese motel in Linchuan. There was such generous ventilation in my room that you could easily winnow corn by holding a basin of it in front of my window. Joseph Wu's brother came to see us. He was a middle school student and the tears came to his eyes as he recalled the pressure that had been put on him to apostatise. He never wavered, however. The next morning, he came at dawn to serve our masses and to receive Holy Communion. As we were leaving the bus station the next day, two old consecrated virgins, who had been catechists in Hsiao Shih and Lichuan, came along to say goodbye and to get our blessings.

Two soldiers accompanied us as escorts from Nancheng to Hong Kong and I must say that they did not bother us all that much. They travelled on the bus with us to Linchuan and next day to Nanchang and brought us to where we should stay the night in each place, and then left. Presumably, they wanted to see the town themselves. We spent a day or two in Nanchang, the capital of the Jiangsi Province. To our great delight, who came to visit us the night we arrived in the capital but a Kiutu girl called She Jen. She was a sister of Wang Bay Hua who was executed by the Communists in Kiutu and she was now a nurse in the capital. She was accompanied by another Catholic girl who had done three months in jail.

She Jen told us that the Archbishop, who was in jail in the capital, was to be seen on many days sweeping the streets of the city. As I have noted, two of his Chinese priests trumped up false charges against him and he got life imprisonment. She Jen was very well instructed and knew that she could not go to confession to these excommunicated priests or receive Holy Communion from them, so we heard her confession and the confession of the other girl and the two girls had only just left when a member of the Nanchang Secret Police entered.

The God of Pleasant Surprises sent us another visitor whom we were delighted to see – none other than our own seminarian Joseph Wu. He was on his way to the seminary in Shanghai on his way to the priesthood. Until we saw him in Nanchang, we had not fully believed he, Tommy and Peter would be allowed to make the journey. The news was too good to be true. We told him that we would be saying Mass about dawn the next morning and that we would be glad if he could attend. We indicated to him that we would like him to take some Sacred Hosts to She Jen so that she and the other Catholic nurses who had not joined the Patriotic Church Movement would be able to receive Holy Communion.

Next morning, we had finished Mass before our military escorts had got up and we had had given Joseph Wu my pyx containing about twelve consecrated hosts, and Seamus's pyz too. The previous day we had explained to She Jen that during the persecution we had faculties to authorise her to give Holy Communion to the other loyal Catholic nurses. We also gave her some brief instructions on how she might reserve the Blessed Sacrament and guard it.

Next day, as we walked through the city of Nanchang we saw quite a few cars whereas the last time we had been there, there were no cars to be seen. We were told that most of these cars belonged to Russian technicians and so forth who were now living in Nanchang. That morning we boarded a train at Nanchang railway station for Changsha. We were interested to note that as we passed each station on our journey south, there was a band waiting with garlands for the Chinese volunteers who had gone to help Korean communists and were expected back.

We got into Changsha at seven o'clock in the evening. A tall blue-coated Red agent made a bee-line for us as soon as he saw us. 'Did you come from Russia?' he asked. 'No,' we answered, 'we came from Nanchang.' In his excitement, he may have convinced himself that we were Russians who were apparently expected in the town and did not hear our reply. Be that as it may, he took my bag, carried it, and led us to the Mandarin's office.

When we arrived at the Mandarin's office we were greeted with great friendliness by the men and women of the staff in the office. Shortly afterward, our blue-coated guide took us up to another office and there they awoke to the fact that we were not Russians, but that we were priests. The tall blue-coat was a bit disconcerted and must have lost quite a bit of face. Still, he took us back to the railway station and there we were able to get two rooms in a motel.

When I was saying Mass about one o'clock that night, Seamus was serving and when he looked out the window, he noticed two strangers arriving at the station. They were met by the bigwigs of the town and obviously they were the Russians for whom our blue-coated friend had been waiting when he spotted us.

We got the train very early that morning on our journey south.

That night we reached Canton and, after much difficulty at the customs, we were fortunate enough to procure one bed. Next morning we took the train from Canton to the Chinese border and there we were met by a Columban, John McNamara and the Hong Kong police, and our escorts turned back to Nancheng. After a short delay at the border we took the train to Kowloon station and then we crossed the ferry and were welcomed warmly by Bishop Cleary and Columban Sister Mercedes. We had a most enjoyable dinner with the Columban Sisters in Ruttonjee Sanatorium and it was great to be back with our own again.

The Bishop was staying at the Maryknoll House, Stanley, in the outskirts of Hong Kong. The Maryknoll Fathers are the National Missionary Society of North America. John McNamara was staying there, and his job was to look after Columbans coming out of China. Most of the Maryknoll priests in Stanley were old China hands, and some of them had been recently expelled. They were all Americans and they received us warmly. I remember their names: Tom Malone, Bill Mulcahy, Maurice Aherne, Joe McGinn, Bishop Paschang, Paul Duchesne, Mark Tennien. Bishop Cleary, Seamus and I had a get together in John McNamara's room to review the Nancheng situation since his expulsion.

Meantime, Bishop Cleary had got all his papers ready and was due to fly out to the U.S.A. en route to Ireland. Seamus and I had a few sessions with him before he left and we went over the Chinese situation again. To have been with him was a blessing and an education. We 'sunged' him to Kai Tak airport in Hong Kong and we missed him very much when he was gone.

Seamus and I were the last two foreign priests in our Diocese of

Nancheng. In our Province of Jiangsi, there were five Catholic dioceses but there was only one foreign priest left in the Province by the time we were sent out. That priest's name was Joe Hill, an American Vincentian, and he arrived in Hong Kong shortly after us.

What happened to Jiangsi province happened in every province all over China and over a year later – in November 1954 – a Sword of the Spirit pamphlet called Religious Freedom in China reported: 'There were nearly 6,000 foreign Catholics missionaries in China, bishops, priests, sisters and religious orders of every nationality before the Reds came. There are, today, only 93 left in the whole of China, 4 bishops, of whom 2 are in jail; 1 prefect apostolic, who is in jail, 62 priests, of whom 20 are in jail, 3 monks and 26 nuns. 39 of the foreign missionaries were killed or died in jail, the remainder were expelled, most of them after months, sometimes years of physical or mental torture in order to make them confess to crimes they never committed'. I wonder, now, if Church history has anything to show which would remotely compare with the rapid devastation of the institutional Catholic Church in China in the few short years from 1949 to 1954.

PART IV:

After We Left

CHAPTER 21

Fearless Faith

The magic carpet which transports us back to China, to the very month Seamus and I left Nancheng, is a letter from China in 1980, a few years after the death of Mao Tse Tung. Fr Jim Yang wrote to Ted MacElroy, then in Hong Kong, and he was asked to send copies to Seamus who was in Derby, New York, and to me. I was in Glasgow.

I shall now quote from the letter: 'After our Bishop and the two O'Reillys left Nancheng, there were only Joe Peng, Paul Yu, and the Vincentian priest from Yu Kiang Diocese, free in the whole district. As a matter of fact, even their freedom was strictly limited, that is, their movement was confined to Nancheng City. Paul Yu was living with his brother, Peter, and looking after his milking cows in order to earn his living as well as to pass the time. Strictly speaking, therefore, Joseph Peng was really the only one taking care of the Catholics. He did excellent work and gained a general high respect from both Christians and pagans.

You probably still remember the old Protestant parson called Lo Mu-Chi who was imprisoned in 1958 and afterwards sentenced to 15 years hard labour. That old friend of ours used to praise Joe Peng highly. Joe really did tremendous work among the Catholics and led them to fight for the freedom of their faith bravely. He gathered the Christians closely around himself so that whenever the government wanted to have a talk with him, the Catholics would not let him go alone.

The climax came one day in 1954. They crowded up in the Hsing Gin Fu demanding to see the respected Fr Joseph Peng immediately. The guards tried to shut them out of the office, but the irritated masses ignored their threats of firing the rifles. As a matter of fact, the more the guards tried to threaten the crowds, the more the latter became angry. Finally, they broke the gate and rushed into the

office. Seeing that they could not do anything with a crowd of nearly a hundred people, including men and women, old and young,
they let Joe Peng come out and he triumphantly led the crowd back
to the church.

This, of course, inflamed the devils with hatred against Joseph
Peng. Therefore, on September 8th, 1955, poor Joe was arrested. He
was jailed in Nancheng for more than half a year and then sentenced to twelve years imprisonment with hard labour. After that
he was sent to a prisoners' farm where he died sometime in 1968.
The exact date of his death is not known for it was not till nearly
two years later that the sad news was heard. Anyhow, it is generally
concluded that he was heavily tortured during the years of the
cultural revolution and it is most likely that the serious suffering
involved caused his death.'

In Columban Mission of August/September 1983, Seamus O'Reilly
has this to say: 'In 1952, during Joe's pre-ordination retreat, the
Bishop asked me to stress strongly as I could the fact that, as a
priest, he would not have an easy life. He would certainly face imprisonment and possibly death. Therefore, he should be completely
certain he wished to be ordained. I shall not forget his reply: 'Tell
the Bishop I do not care how long or how short I live as a priest,
whether it is six months or six years, if I can do something for God
and for the Church I shall die happy.'

During my last two years in Nancheng, 1950-1952, I was fairly frequently summoned to appear before one or other of the communist
bigwigs and the bishop always would send Joe Peng or Tommy Yu
to accompany me. The communist bigwigs would get angry, and
when you are living in a very tense atmosphere, and under-
nourished, it is easy to get excited yourself. I found myself rejecting
their false charges with vigour and witnessing to our faith in like
manner.

Generally on our way back to the compound, a bout of remorse
would hit me. I would blame myself for not having answered them
meekly and mildly, realising with hindsight that a more gentle
approach would make things easier for Joe Peng and Tommy Yu in
the future. After all, the communists regarded me as a criminal and
they could accuse Joe and Tommy of associating with a criminal
and co-operating with him. Why did I not tone things down a bit? I

asked myself, seeing that they came from a young Christianity whereas we foreigners came from older Christianities. I now see that my thinking was both presumptuous and patronising. I was saying that we can take it but the Chinese cannot.

One night, after I got the letter, I was doing my spiritual reading in the little oratory of the Columban house in Glasgow, and the reading included the following (Matthew 10:19-20): 'You will be dragged before Governors and Kings for my sake to bear testimony before them and the gentiles. When they deliver you up, do not be anxious how you are to speak or what you are to say, for what you are to say will be given to you in that hour; for it is not you who speaks but the Spirit of your Father speaking through you.'

The words leaped at me from the page. Honestly, I never noticed before that night that the passage contained the words, 'how you are to speak'. What I had felt guilty about, over the years, was that I had shouted at the Communist chief of police. I feared that this would be held against Joe in years to come. Now I believed for the first time that the Holy Spirit was using me, not only in what I said but in the way I said it, to prepare Joe and to rehearse with him for the ordeals he had to face after we had left China.I am afraid I cried like a child as I thought of Joe Peng and me being brought before the bigwigs in 1951 and 1952 and Joe subsequently being brought before the communist police and being tortured, after we were expelled.

But what had Jim's letter to say about the three seminarians who were scheduled to go tothe seminary in Shanghai?

By the summer of 1954, the three seminarians were back in Nancheng and had been in jail for a while.

In the spring of 1957, the three of them, Tommy Yu, Joseph Wu and Peter Hsieh, were ordained by Archbishop Chou of Nanchang who had been released shortly before that. However, there were problems because one of the schismatic priests threatened to beat up some of the Nancheng Chinese priests unless he himself was allowed to assist at the ordination ceremony. Archbishop Chou solved the dilemma by saying that he, the ordaining prelate, would perform the ceremony without any assistance from any other priest. After the ordination, the three young priests returned to Nancheng.

I quote here from the letter: 'Thanks be to God and the Queen of the Holy Rosary, three young priests of God ascended at last to the altar of Our Lord to offer Christ the Divine Victim to our Almighty God and Father for the salvation of souls. All the good Catholics were delighted to see their own sons raised to the height of the priesthood. They also considered this success as a triumphant victory of the Diocese and especially of Our Lady of the Holy Rosary.

The Easter of 1957 was really a glorious feast for us. There were seven priests in Nancheng and we performed all the ceremonies with our traditional solemnity as far as we could do so, as we still had the chapel and the convent. Though we were not able to do much outside of Nancheng, some Catholics came from the neighbourhood such as Kiutu, Chuliang, Pakan etc., but this, of course, made the schismatic Patriotic Church Catholics feel envy at the good Catholics, because the patriotic church people, although they were able to attend the Masses, were not admitted to receive the sacraments. Jealousy is one of the sources of evil, as is known to all.'

Towards the end of April, Jim Yang, Paul Yu and Tommy Yu went to Shanghai to Our Lady's shrine at Szoshan. Jim Yang said Mass on the main altar on the 1st of May and offered the Diocese once more to Our Blessed Lady entreating her to give a special protection under her powerful cloak to priests and people. I quote again from the letter: 'There was going to be a solemn celebration that day but because we had some appointment in Shanghai, we returned to the city immediately after breakfast without taking part in the public celebration. Another reason, and the main reason too, was that there were some Patriotic Church priests trying to mess up the good event. We stole back to Rue Maresca, that is, the Columban House.'

Starting on the Feast of Christ the King, towards the end of that same October 1957, the priests were again put in jail.

'Our three young priests have proved to be excellent all this time. They all stood firmly against the enemies. They were arrested one after another between the winter of 1957 and the summer of 1958, and every one of them was sentenced to more than ten years imprisonment and they all served it without complaint. When this term of imprisonment was over, Peter Hsieh was released and sent back to Nanfeng where he lived with his brother and worked as a cook in a small inn in the village in order to earn a bit of money to support himself. Last summer when the label of 'reactionary' was taken off, he was freed and in the autumn he was asked to teach English in a middle school in the city. Even though he had forgotten a lot of his English, he was still appointed to teach the advanced classes in the school, but being a Catholic priest, he was not fairly treated regarding the wages. Up to this summer, he was able to run about between Nanfeng and Nancheng and he has done fine work there.

Since the Patriotic Church Movement has been backed up by the government to revive their work again, Peter was warned to keep himself quiet, otherwise, he would get into trouble and Catholics would be forced again to join the Patriotic Church Movement both in Nanfeng and Nancheng. They had already started such dirty work a few months earlier. Joseph Wu and Tommy Yu had been put together in the same farm for prisoners. The term of their imprisonment had been over several years, but they were kept as farm workers. Owing to his poor health, Joseph Wu was dismissed and they let him go home last summer.

Shortly after he went home, he got a job in a College of Education in Fuchow teaching English. The College was quite satisfied with his work and he was well respected by the students and as the Catholics of Fuchow were so good and so many, he was often asked to hear confessions and say Mass and administer the sacraments.

The priests and Catholics of Fuchow made a good preparation for the Feast of Pentecost. In order to prevent the solemn celebration of the Feast, the Government did not let Fr Tseu, who was living in the countryside, come to the city and they sent Joseph Wu to Kukiang to attend some special lectures. Thus they tried to impede the celebration to take place. Of course, they did not fully succeed though Joe was not able to take part in the celebration. The demons were not satisfied with this.

Sometime after the feast, the head of the Patriotic Church Movement in Nanchang went to Fuchow trying to stop the activities of the Catholics there. The first thing they did was to urge the college to dismiss Joseph Wu; the college did it on the grounds that Joseph had refused to join the Patriotic Church Movement. Thanks be to

God, Joseph got another job in a middle school. I met him yesterday in the city and we had dinner together. He told me has has been asked to by another college to teach there and is doing well in his new post.

Tommy Yu had been regarded as the pride of the Diocese but the hatred of the enemies. Because he is the most active of the three he has been refused by the police bureau to let him go back to Pakan and live in his elder sister's house. He has been arrested twice and sentenced to imprisonment twice. The first time during his imprisonment, on account of his outstanding heroic action in saving another man's life by running the risk of sacrificing his own, the government released him three years before the term was up, that is, in 1964. He stayed with his sister in Pakan under close surveillance by the Reds, doing farmwork to earn his living. Meanwhile, he was pretty active and a good number of Catholics went to see him and this, of course, infuriated the fiends, and he was again accused in 1966 of having spread Catholicism which was considered by them reactionary. He was sentenced to ten years imprisonment once more and was sent to this place labouring together with me in the same workshop. In 1968 he was sent to a prisoners' farm where he spent twelve years. The labour is very hard and heavy, especially for a man over fifty; his older sister and himself have tried their best to get him out of the abyss of misery, but they failed. As I, myself, am in the same position as Tommy, I cannot do anything for him and admit my ability falling short of my wishes. However, he is very optimistic and is keeping himself always in good form and his good humour and generosity gain for him a good opinion wherever he goes. He has not failed to live up to the teaching of Our Lord to be the salt of the earth and the light of the world.'

I know, but I haven't any documentary evidence now, that when Tommy was in Pakan he went down regularly to say Mass in Kiutu, his parish, about ten miles away, at night. Apparently the communist spies caught him saying Mass in some Catholic's house and he was given the heavy sentence to which Jim Yang refers in his letter.

At a conference on Christianity in China held in the London area in 1985, at which all Christian denominations were represented, I met a nice young man from Amnesty International and he told me that Amnesty would do anything possible to get Tommy Yu released. I conveyed this information to Sr Teresita Yu with whom I have been corresponding regularly over the years. A few months later, that nice young Manchester man made a trip to Hong Kong and visited Sr Teresita. We also, all the Nancheng sisters and priests, have been praying over the years for all the priests but especially for Tommy. Fancy my indescribable delight when Columban Sr Maureen McGinley told me on the telephone that Tommy had been released. Amnesty International played a part in getting him released, no doubt. On July 20th 1988, I received confirmation from Hong Kong about Tommy's release - the letter was from Sr Teresita Yu and she gave quite a few details. She said that, despite all that Tommy has suffered over the long years in jail, his health was not nearly so bad as one would have expected.

The first Chinese priest to die was Fr John Chang. He was put in jail in 1952 and then released in 1954 because of chronic tuberculosis. He was allowed to return to his mother's home where he died in 1959. Fr John had surprised us all at a farewell supper the night before our public trial in February 1952. After we had toasted the Church in China and the Holy Father, John got to his feet and sang, in a weak and quavering voice, 'Christus vincit, Christus regnat, Christus imperat!' – Christ conquers, Christ reigns, Christ rules. As Seamus ended his telling of this story in 'Columban Mission', 'Christ conquered in Fr John in spite of fear and terror; he went manfully to prison the next day.'

Fr Phil Chou was in the parish of Hengstun, near Lichwan, and I often met him in Nancheng when I was in Kiutu. Jim's letter says of Phil, 'It appears that for the last ten or twelve years of his life he was imprisoned in his own house and held under close surveillance by the communists. He had a very hard life and it is generally thought that he died from starvation, for even though some good Catholics risked being caught to give him some money or some food, the poor man dared not receive it.'

There are two more of the Chinese priests whose stories I have not yet told. One of them, Luke Teng, was put to jail shortly after I was expelled from Kiutu and he was released three years later and was in Nancheng until he was re-arrested in 1958. He and Paul Yu, who was living with us in Nancheng before the bishop was expelled, were arrested together. I shall now quote from the letter we received from Jim Yang: 'Fr Teng and Fr Yu were sent to a prisoners' farm not far from Po Yang lake after being sentenced to ten or fifteen years imprisonment. The date of their death is not known for certain but according to the general opinion they both died not too long after they had been sent there. Luke Teng had high blood pressure while Paul Yu had constant trouble with his stomach.

In the years between 1959 and 1961, the whole country was stricken by starvation, hence it was quite a common occurrence that prisoners died from hunger or from illness caused by hunger. Luke Teng and Paul Yu were probably some of the victims of that terrible famine. They were both the pride of our diocese. Paul Yu was appointed Vicar General of Nanchang Diocese by Archbishop Chou in 1957, but unfortunately Paul was put in jail before he could take over the job and died before the Archbishop. I hope I may get more details about them before they died in the farm. It is absolutely certain that they stuck to their faith sternly to the end of their lives.'

The other Chinese priest is the writer of the letter, Fr Jim Yang, the Vicar General of the Diocese. In the letter, he wrote: 'I was taken from Nancheng to Nanchang in 1954, after two years in prison in the local jail. It was the Feast of St. Joseph, i.e 19th March 1954, that I was put in a jeep and taken to Nanchang to the higher provincial police officers custody, where they tried to make me yield to their will by means of both hard and soft tactics.

On April 16th, 1955, the Feast of St Bernadette and the anniversary of Bishop Cleary's consecration, I was taken back to Nancheng unexpectedly. For several days in that period, they told me they intended to send me home, provided I would not be stubborn – I should treat the Patriotic Church members the same as the Catholics, restoring them to the right to receive the sacraments, but every time the reply they got was a firm and negative one. I told them again and again that I had done nothing to deserve a punishment, but they considered that I should be punished for having refused to join the Patriotic Church Movement, for having dissuaded Catholics from joining the same, for having denied the accusation against Bishop Cleary and the Church in general, and for having denied the sacraments to those who had joined the Patriotic Church.

I told them, too, that I treasured my freedom but that I would not barter any principles for it, hence if they considered that they should set me free I warned them that I would go back and act exactly the same as I had done before. On the other hand, I stressed the point that I would rather stay in prison till the end of my life than carry out their evil wishes. My stubborn attitude irritated them but at the same time, they could not do anything else but send me home because I believe they had some instructions from above to release me on April 16th. 1955. Having been scolded and abused for more than two hours, I was taken back to Nancheng police bureau where I was told to go back to the church myself.'

Towards the middle of 1957, the People's Political Consultative Conference in Fuchow, about forty or fifty miles from Nancheng, invited Jim to join their Conference and to become Vice Chairman. They promised him that they would restore all properties belonging to the Church and would give some money for the repairs on one condition: the condition, of course, being that the Patriotic Church people would be allowed to receive the sacraments. They reminded Jim that as Vicar of the diocese he should be anxious for the salvation of the souls of the Patriotic Church people. This sounded funny to Jim, coming as it did from atheists, and he laughed, but he told them that he could not do anything to reconcile them to the church unless they took the first step themselves and he again made clear to them the Church's teaching on the matter.

In the middle of August 1957, Jim went to Kwang Chang to bury his brother who was working there in a hospital and who died while on duty. Jim seized the opportunity to visit the Catholics there. Kwang Chang was the parish where Con O'Connell and Pat Gately served before their expulsion. Jim was able to find only a few old ladies. A good number of the old Catholics had died or left the place and some of the youngsters had ceased to practise their religion. He stayed there for several days and met less than ten Catholics in all. Just like the Catholics in some other places, they were very much afraid of approaching their priests at that particular time.

Jim was jailed again on Christmas Eve, 1959, and returned to the same labour camp.

He says in the letter that he met some Catholics in jail and in the labour camp and that they gave outstanding witness to their faith. In fact, some of them were tortured during the cultural revolution.

What surprises me is that he makes no mention of 'John McCormack', although he does mention other Catechists whom he had met in jail. John was our star catechist in Nancheng diocese and he was the only lay person who was tried with the Bishop and us priests and he was jailed the same day as Jim Yang and John Chang. The story I have heard is that he died in jail and that he was tortured, but he died, I seem to remember, a short time after they were all jailed in Nancheng - after our big trial in 1952.

'On January 6th 1960 - (I continue to quote from Jim's letter) - I was taken from Fuchow jail to be remoulded, as they call it, under the penal servitude. Due to the terrible weakness of my poor health I had to be sent to a hospital of the prison to get treatment the day after I came here. The good Catholic, Wu Teng, a prisoner too, was the chief doctor of the clinic and he gave me the treatment. I was absolutely dying but under Dr Teng's good care, my health was gradually restored. I stayed in the hospital for more than two months and since then I have been working in this laboratory as an organic analyst of the materials used in this factory. In 1974 the term of my imprisonment was up but I have been kept to do the analytical work for the factory as before. In the spring of last year (I think last year would mean 1978 or 1979), I was asked to teach English in the local TV university. The complete course was only three terms and no freshmen were accepted this term, therefore, I am not doing any regular teaching work now. I have been trying to get out of this cage but through the apprehensions and suspicions against me our 'friends' would not give me the green light to leave here.

As happened in the case of Tommy Yu, the police bureau of my native town refused to let me go back and live permanently with my nephews. It is not for my own good that I wish to get out of this place but for the benefit of the people, so if I could leave the cage I would be able to do more for our Catholic people. However, 'fiat voluntas tua'. The Catholics here are really like a flock without a shepherd, some are very fervent especially the old people. There is a Patriotic Church priest here but the good Catholics all ignore him. Since 1975, I have started to visit them but because some of them have been frightened they dare not profess their religion openly and also, I cannot do anything for them as my freedom is still limited and I can only see them on rare occasions. How sad it is to see good Catholics longing for the sacraments so eagerly.'

Jim's fears that future sufferings lay ahead of him and his confreres from the Patriotic Church were well-founded because in November 1981, Jim and Tommy Yu and Joseph Wu were jailed again. Joseph Wu died shortly after being imprisoned in the month of January 1982.

Over a year later I had a letter from Sister Teresita Yu. Her letter went: 'Fr Jim is dying of cancer in a hospital to which he has been transferred. No one is allowed to visit him or take him anything. It is terrible; pray for him and for the other priests and people. He is getting only herbal treatment'.

Jim Yang did not, in fact, die. A few weeks ago (September 1988), when I got notification that Tommy Yu had been released, I also learned that Jim Yang had left the hospital in Nancheng and is now living with a relative there but is under some form of house arrest and he is in good form, although he still has the cancer. So Jim and Tommy Yu are both in the Nancheng area and have been able to meet, hopefully, and have a certain amount of freedom. That they got together, discussed things, shared experiences and that Jim 'passed on the torch' to Tommy, who was next in the chain of command, was beautiful.

Jim Yang knew that the Church had made a number of mistakes in its efforts to evangelise China, but he was also intelligent enough to realise there is a human factor in the Church and that as long as fallible human beings are running the Church, so to speak, mistakes will be made.

The other secular priest from Nancheng diocese still alive is Peter Hsieh. He has moved from the Nanfeng area to the Nancheng area but I have no news as to whether he is under control still or what he is doing; presumably he is still under control.

In the letter, Jim Yang tells us about the parishes he tried to visit and I just have just one bit of information to add to what he has given us. A Columban Sister based in Hong Kong wrote to me in November 1986 and she told me that the Patriotic Church Movement sent a Patriotic Church priest to open a church in Kiutu a year earlier but nobody attended so they closed it down. The letter went on to say that the people were praying in their home. When I got the news, the response in my heart was 'Blessed be God forever'.

CHAPTER 22

Roll Call

When we received Jim Yang's letter, Bishop Cleary had been dead about ten years. He died on the 23rd October 1970. Jim's letter was a roll call of all our Chinese priests living and dead who had been left behind us in China in 1953. It was a roll of honour.

At this stage of the story, I must make a roll call of the Columbans, the dead and the living, who left Nancheng in the early fifties.

Seamus and I saw off Bishop Cleary who was flying to the United States from Kaitak Airport, Hong Kong, in March 1953. But what was he up to between that date and his death in 1970 is a question which I must now address. Well, he visited our Columban headquarters in Nebraska and also some of our other Columban houses and also visited friends and relatives in the United States. After that, he returned to Ireland and visited his home and family – the first visit since 1931. He stayed that summer of 1954 in the Columban Sisters' Convent in Cahircon near his own home in County Clare.

By September, he was back in our seminary, St Columban's College, Dalgan Park, Navan, and he taught some classes in New Testament to the seminarians each week. As well as that, he was sometimes invited to administer the Sacrament of Confirmation by some of the Irish bishops and sometimes he was invited to administer the Sacrament of Holy Orders at different colleges or seminaries.

When I was appointed to Ireland in 1961, I lived in our Administration House, now called Blowick House, about a half a mile from the seminary where he lived. I visited him two nights a week, whenever I could manage it, and the visits were very entertaining. The latest news from China we would always discuss and try to figure out how it might affect the Church there. But he also talked about loftier subjects like the latest trends in theology and scripture, and kept up his reading. He also loved small talk and expected me to bring him news of what was happening in all the places I visited, and any funny stories picked up in such places.

From 1963 to 1965, he attended the Second Vatican Council in Rome. He not only attended, but he made an intervention. He was highly amused when a bishop, whom he had taught when he was professor in Maynooth, criticised the theme of his speech saying that it smacked of liberalism.

After the Vatican Council, he slowed down a bit, but he never lost his interest in the seminary and liked to mix with the boys. He had the gift of relating to them in an easy informal manner. He realised that there was quite a bit of confusion in the Church after Vatican II and especially in seminaries. He said to me, more than once, ruefully, 'If they ever lose the Dalgan spirit, I'll turn in my grave.' The 'Dalgan spirit' was what he tried to instill into the seminarians in our first seminary, St Columban's, Dalgan Park, Galway, and he tried to instill that same spirit into the seminarians whom he taught in China and who witnessed so heroically during the persecution.

I visited him every day during his last illness, and the night before he died, he said to me, 'I am a bad patient' and laughed merrily.

These words from Jim Yang's letter to Ted MacElroy must surely be his most fitting epitaph: 'Let the Holy Father know that though small and unknown to fame as our diocese is, there are in it four priests fighting bravely for their faith. They have refused to join the Patriotic Church at the loss of their freedom for more than twenty-five years. In fact, five of their comrades in arms have already offered their lives for the same cause. Dear Father, I want you to do this for us, not because we have anything worthy to make a boast of, but we wish to let the Holy See know that we are not unworthy to be the children of St Columban's and that the apostolic work of our most respected and beloved Bishop Cleary has definitely brought forth its fruit.' Remember, that letter was written nearly thirty years after we left China.

About three months after Bishop Cleary's death, Frank Whelan, who was pastor in Lichuan, died at St Columban's, Nebraska, on the 18th January, 1971. Frank and his curate, Peter Campbell, were tried and expelled from Lichuan on 17th March 1951. They were sent under escort direct to Hong Kong and were not allowed to stay a night with us in Nancheng. Frank was very pleasant, gentle and a very good singer. After his expulsion, he was appointed to St Columban's, Nebraska, where he became the General Office Manager. Frank was one of five priest-brothers, three of whom were Columbans. Joe is a Columban and he is retired here in St Columban's, Navan – the last of the five brothers.

And then on the 10th July 1975, we got the sad news that Mike Halford had died in Florida where he had been doing parish work for some time. It was joyful news too, because Mike had been suffering for quite a time from very painful cancer. Since he left China, Mike had been teaching in a few of our colleges there and the testimony of the American Columbans whom he taught was that he was an excellent teacher. Though we corresponded regularly and I am very sorry I did not keep his letters, they were so funny, the last time we met was in 1954. Just before the All-Ireland Final that year, he alerted me to the fact that he was in Ireland and invited me to join him at the match. His native County, Meath, won the All-Ireland and we were overjoyed. In those days, the crowd sang 'Faith of our Fathers' at All-Ireland Football Finals and Hurling Finals too. It was a moving experience for Mike and me to stand up with the fifty or sixty thousand and sing with them 'Faith of our Fathers, Holy Faith, We will be true to thee till death.' As we sang, our minds raced back to that night in Kiutu in 1950 when we sang the Divine Praises after Fr Theunisson's death. I often feel that Mike had a more painful death than Fr Theunisson but I am sure he offered the pain for the Catholics in his parish and the diocese whom he had served so well.

It was with deep shock we learned of Ted MacElroy's unexpected death in Hong Kong on the 22nd November 1980. Ted was a priest of Nancheng diocese but he became Director of a region of China which included Hanyang diocese, Nancheng diocese and Hochow district. He did his best for the Columbans in these areas and he was instrumental in getting our three seminarians into the seminary in Shanghai in 1953. In 1954, he was expelled from China and after that he went to England and directed the Emigrant Chaplains Apostolate. In 1963, he went to Lima, Peru, and in 1974, he was appointed to Hong Kong where he looked after the affairs of our priests in Burma, because they were going through a very difficult period. He flew in food and other necessities of life to those suffering priests. As well as that he did his best to keep in touch with our Chinese priests and Catholics in the districts staffed by the Columbans. A sad sequel to Ted's death was that a day or two after he died, Jim Yang sent him two flasks of Chinese wine in rare Chinese wood and beautifully decorated. One of the flasks was for Ted and the other was for me. Ted would have been very touched at Jim's thoughtfulness in spite of his sufferings and trials and what you could call martyrdom in slow motion over the years.

When I got the news of Barney O'Neill's death on the Feast of the Epiphany, 1986, I felt a great sense of loss. Barney had suffered a lot of mental anguish and humiliation when he pleaded my case before the Commissar when I was charged with sabotaging the revolution. Between his expulsion from China and his death, he worked in Ireland. Most of it was on missionary awareness, promotion work, but also he was Bursar for a period. He was courteous, kind, hard-working and completely without guile.

In that same year, 1986, Pat Gately died on the 14th April in Los Angeles. After his expulsion from China, he worked on missionary awareness in the United States, as a hospital chaplain and on pastoral work. I visited him in hospital in Los Angeles less than a year before his death. Although he was ill, he recalled a number of amusing incidents from the days when he was rector of the major seminary in Nancheng and where I was on the staff for a year before the Reds came. His laughter was not as high-powered as it had been thirty years earlier, but he chuckled with amusement as he reminisced there in his sick bed.

But more sad news was in store for us, when we got word of Peter Campbell's death on 28th December 1987. Our friendship was close and it went back to our seminary days where he was a class after me. We both played for the Dalgan Gaelic Football team. Peter played for his native County Tyrone and also for Ulster and was one of the greats in Gaelic football in his day. We talked Irish in the same group in Dalgan also, and after ordination, he served in Birmingham city during World War II. He succeeded me in Lichuan as curate in 1947. After his expulsion from China in 1951, he was assigned to promotion work, as we called it then, or missionary awareness, as we call it now, in the United States. He was rector in our house in Brooklyn and our house in New York, and later worked in Westchester, Pennsylvania. In 1969, he went to the Philippines as a missionary but, after a few years, his health began to deteriorate and he returned to Ireland. I am so glad I visited him in Maghery on the shores of Lough Neagh where he had a very nice church and residence, in the summer of 1986. Although he had a heart ailment, he sparkled that night as he recalled the China days and the Dalgan days. He recalled that when he entered Dalgan in 1935, everybody seemed to have a spring in the step and a song in the heart. But the society was young in those days and its members were young, and youth in the organisation and in the personnel is a formidable combination.

I fear that in my roll call of deceased Columban priests who have served in Nancheng during the persecution the first shall be last. Actually, Mick Moran was the first to die and he died at his own home in Glencorrib, Co Mayo on New Year's Day in 1954. He was only fifty-three years old. After his expulsion from China, he returned to Ireland for his first holiday since he left home twenty-four years earlier. After his holiday, he became a curate in Craughwell, Co Galway.

When we were criminals together in Nancheng, he got up at about 4.30 each morning and spent four to five hours in the presence of the Blessed Sacrament. He was very good with his hands and quite a carpenter. Before his expulsion from his parish, he frequently made coffins for the destitute non-believers and believers. He had a good sense of humour and gave rein to it in the steady flow of articles he wrote for the 'Far East' from his parish in Nancheng. Carrying wood and drawing water I found rather boring, so I asked Mick, the pig supremo, to give me a job as a casual pig waiter, taking the pigs their breakfast, supper and tea. As his part-time assistant, I found more fulfilment and job satisfaction and even a certain amount of vanity showed when the pigs responded so promptly as I intoned the Chinese pig call either at morning, noon or evening. When I was promoted to casual pig waiter, I fear it was said that the promotion was due to 'pull' or 'the old school tie' because Mick and I had both been pupils at St Jarlath's, Tuam. Mick was fourteen years older than I was.

Just as I read the page-proofs of this book, in December 1990, Pat Dermody and Hugh Bennett both died here in Dalgan. Pat was V.G. in Nancheng for a number of years. In his thirty years in China, he lived under the communists three times. The first time was in Hanyang in the mid-twenties and he had to go on the run because of the danger of being captured. He accompanied Fr Tierney when the Columbans took over Nancheng mission. Tim Leonard was killed the year after, 1929, and it was Pat Dermody who recovered the body and buried him. The communists stayed in the Nancheng area until 1934 when the Long March started, and after that Pat lived under the communists again from 1949 to 1951. After his expulsion from China, he served in Los Angeles for over twenty years and then took a chaplaincy in Ireland.

Hugh Bennett was well up in his eighties when he died. He was a late vocation, a native of Liverpool and had been a tailor by trade before deciding to become a missionary. He also had played for an English football team, West Bromwich Albion. As a student, he played handball with Fr John Blowick, our co-founder. Fr John told me in a very entertaining manner about the handball matches they had together. After his expulsion from China, Hugh helped his friend, Bishop Heenan, in the diocese of Leeds. He was a curate in St Mary's, Bradford, when I made a missionary appeal in that parish. Later he became parish priest in Settle in the Yorkshire Dales and after that he came to Warrenpoint as chaplain to the Alexian Brothers Nursing Home.

Joe Flynn was appointed Dalgan Park after he returned from China. He became rector seven or eight years later. After he finished his term as rector, Joe continued to teach theology and Canon Law as he has a doctorate in both disciplines. After Ted MacElroy's death, he was sent to Hong Kong to keep in touch with our Chinese priests and Catholics to the best of his ability. He also helped a lot in the Curial office in Hong Kong where his knowledge of Canon Law was put to practical use. He is now doing pastoral work in a parish in Ireland and still keeps up his golf.

Of the three Nancheng priests who went to Japan, one, Pat Sheehy, is now back in Ireland since the summer of 1989 and is doing pastoral work. He was very good at the Japanese languages as those of us who knew him in China would expect. He checked my story, especially the parts of it where he was personally involved. He has a very good memory and still remembers quite a bit of the Chinese language. The other two priests who went from Nancheng to Japan are Tom Fisher and Vincent McNally. Tom was appointed to England in the seventies and became pastor of a parish we staff in Widnes. He invited me to Widnes to give a day of renewal to the priests of the Widnes area before the visit of Pope John Paul II to England. We had a very enjoyable couple of days together and he is still very young in mind and heart.

Vincent McNally and I have met very little in the last thirty years, though we were quite close friends in China. I believe I did meet him in Kumomoto, Japan, when I flew over from Seoul, where I was giving a retreat to the Columbans in Korea in 1972. Of all the priests who came to China after the war, I think Vincent was the best at the language in our diocese. I hear he is equally good at Japanese. He does not play the melodeon now as he did in China but as in his Chinese days, he still smokes the pipe. He is the same gentle, humble person as he was in our days in Nancheng.

Con O'Connell was the only one of the Nancheng missionaries who was sent to the Philippines after his expulsion. He has worked very hard in the Philippines and has done quite a lot of building and of church repairs. I had a long session with him when I was giving a retreat to our priests in the Philippines in 1971 and found him full of health and full of good humour, as he always had been. Con fought a burst appendix on his feet in 1929 and only learned that he had suffered from that complaint when he was being operated for gall stones in San Francisco in 1955. Con did admit that he did have discomfort and pain on his right side away back but that he was very busy and he just carried on.

Of the eight Columbans left, I suppose Seamus O'Reilly is the one whom I have been in closest contact with since our China days. In 1956/57, we worked together in London, Southwark diocese, on missionary awareness. After a year he moved to the United States to do the same work as he had been doing in England. After I was appointed to Glasgow in 1978, Seamus visited me each year on his way to Ireland for his annual holiday. He was rector in the Retreat House run by the Columbans in Derby-on-the-Lake near Buffalo and he invited me out one autumn to give the annual retreat to the Columbans in the New York and Boston area. We had a very enjoyable trip down to Boston and Bristol, Rhode Island, from Derby-on-the-Lake when the retreat was over. He was in big demand as a retreat master both for priests and people in the United States. In Easter of 1984, we met by chance in Assissi. He had come from the States to Rome and I had been chaplain to a group of Glasgow Catholics as they wanted to be in Rome for Easter. When we got back to Rome from Assisi we had a great evening together and Seamus had a pass which entitled him to say Mass on the High Altar at St Peter's the next day. He invited me to come along with him. I had already arranged to say Mass for my pilgrims from Glasgow on that day, but I had told them that we would have Mass at a quiet side altar in a dignitary-free zone in the Basilica. The pass took us all the way to the sacristy where twenty to thirty clergymen were vested for a concelebrated Mass on the High Altar. To my consternation, the sacristan came over to me when I was vested and pointed to the High Altar and told me that I was to do Chief Concelebrant. As he told me, he seem to give me an impervious stare. But then I nearly panicked and looked beseechingly at Seamus for help but I could see that he was laughing inwardly for all his worth. The Glasgow pilgrims laughed outwardly after the Mass and asked me if I had got advancement in the Church during the evening as I had not told them that I was to do Chief Concelebrant in St Peter's High Altar. I was overawed by the surroundings, Bernini's colonnade and so on, but that Mass left no impression on me at all compared to some of the Masses I said during the persecution.

As I am now coming to the end of my roll call, I must salute the Columban Sisters who served with us in Nancheng under the communists and through part of the persecution. Their contribution is invaluable. Sr Attracta Egan was matron of the hospital and it was she who sent me the ultimate anti-snake deterent when I was on the run on the hills. It was Sr Baptist Connolly, the sister in charge, who realised that when we priests were summoned before the communists to answer false charges that Thung Gwa was our secret weapon. She made sure that he was kneeling before the Blessed Sacrament before and during our ordeals. Thung Gwa was very close to God and God only knows all we owe to his prayers. Some said Thung Gwa was not the full shilling, some said he was the full shilling during inflation, but all recognised that he was our man of prayer, our man of God. Sr Baptist was a native Irish speaker and had known and spoken to Pádraic Pearse as a child when he came to his cottage in Rosmuc to learn Irish. Then there was Sr

Malachy McPolin who visited the Catholics in their homes, specially the sick and the palsied, and also instructed some of the Chinese women who wanted to be received into the Church. The communists were very impressed with the compassion and understanding with which Sr Berchmans Dooley ran the orphanage and the old people's home in our compound. Then there was Sr Frances Monaghan who, amongst other things, trained Chinese girls from outlying parishes to cook and to make bread and the girls trained by her would look after the cooking in the different compounds in the diocese. In times of crises, the Sisters showed an unexpected resilience, inner reserves of strength and an ability to cope which was surprising. From their contacts with other Catholic women and partly from their intuitions, they seem to have much better information regarding what was going on than we priests had. Of the sisters I have named, only Sr Berchmans and Sr Frances are still alive. Sr Attracta died in December 1989, but the other two are dead for quite some time.

Whenever I read in my breviary the inspired words, 'As they go through the Bitter Valley, they make it a place of springs' (Psalm 83), I think of the sisters, the Chinese and foreign priests, who went through the 'bitter valley' of Red persecution. Their strong faith, their unfaltering hope, their Christian joy, made the bitterness tolerable and sometimes even sweet. In the very many churches we priests preached in, Sunday after Sunday, we asked for the prayers and the sufferings of the people for the Catholics in Nancheng. Always, we were back with these persecuted Catholics in spirit, but Seamus was the one who went back in the flesh.

EPILOGUE

Back to China

Seamus flew out from Hong Kong to Nanchang via Canton on 26th October 1988. After his return from China he sent me a very comprehensive, perceptive and most interesting report on his journey. In both Nanchang and Canton he did not sense the slightest trace of Marxism in the atmosphere, but felt that, apart from a government that proclaimed Marxism, the people were not socialist but out and out capitalist. He goes on, and I quote, 'By nature the Chinese seem to be the most capitalistic of all people, their genetic code must have a capitalistic gene which other people lack. Now that the government permits private business ventures, the people are responding whole-heartedly and doing what they know best – making a profit. Poor Karl Marx.'

Seamus was accompanied by Tommy Murphy, a young Columban who is working in Taiwan and whose Chinese is very good. When they reached Nanchang, they tried to contact Fr Tommy Yu from their hotel. They heard in Hong Kong that Tommy was staying in the Catholic Church in Nanchang where there was a Patriotic Church bishop living, when Tommy had been taken there from prison. Tommy informed the officials that he would not join the Patriotic Association, that he had gone to prison several times in the past rather than do so, and that he was willing to go back to prison if necessary rather than join it. The officials assured him that he did not have to join the Patriotic Church and that he was free to carry out his priestly duties. Tommy Yu invited Seamus and Tommy Murphy to a 7.30 a.m. Mass next morning, which was the Feast of Christ the King and the Mass was to take place in a church attached to the convent of a congregation of Chinese sisters. Tommy and Seamus turned up at 7.30 and the congregation were mostly women, but there were men too and they chanted their prayers in Chinese as they had done when we were there. The Mass was in Latin, of course. Seamus listened to Tommy's sermon and in his report he says, 'Given the place and the situation and the man, the sermon was superb. It was a magnificent proclamation of the Catholic faith which he had held and for which he was imprisoned for nearly thirty years. There were about one hundred people present at the Mass, and some of them were young too and some of them country people. A large number received Holy Communion and, at the conclusion of Mass, they had Benediction of the Blessed Sacrament with three hymns in Latin, the *Salve Regina, O Salutaris Hostia* and *Tantum Ergo*, and two hymns in Chinese.'

That same morning, the Feast of Christ the King, Seamus and Tommy Murphy hired a taxi to take them the hundred mile journey to Nancheng and they hoped to continue to Nanfeng. Seamus found that the road to Nancheng was a good highway and it enabled them to make good time. It was a big improvement on the old days when there was only a gravel road for travellers.

The main objective of Seamus's visit to Nancheng, and indeed to China, was to see Jim Yang, the V.G. of the diocese, who had given such heroic and outstanding leadership during the persecution. Unfortunately he was not allowed. The public security bureau man told Seamus that he was 'Lai sen fu' and that he had been in China years earlier. The two priests were greatly surprised and the officials seemed very pleased when Seamus told them of the improvement in the roads and of the fact that the people seemed well fed. The priests were in for another surprise when the officer told Seamus that he, Seamus, knew Fr Yang. Then he explained that Fr Yang was a criminal and that the government had released him so that he could have medical care at home. He warned Seamus that if he insisted on going to see Fr Yang, there would be consequences for Fr Yang's family and for Seamus too. They hated Jim Yang because they failed to make him join the Patriotic Church. When Jim Yang heard Seamus was coming to Nancheng, he expressed an ardent wish to meet him, but the communists denied his wish although he was dying.

Seamus goes on to say that his heart sunk when he saw our Cathedral; the doors were locked, some windows were broken, the roof was damaged. All he could think of was Joyce Kilmer's beautiful poem, 'The House with Nobody in it' and its concluding lines, 'But a house with nobody in it is a house with a broken heart.' Originally,

the Cathedral stood well back from the street in the Church compound, but when they widened the street, a lot of the entrance way
had been taken away so that there was a very short distance from
the street to the steps leading up to the church. Seamus felt
depressed but he was really horrified when he discovered that the
little Church in the Columban Sisters' compound had been turned
into the local abortion centre where all the forced abortions were
performed.

From Nancheng, Seamus and Tommy drove to Chuliang, ten miles
south, where Seamus had been pastor for a few years during the
persecutions. The church school buildings which were being util-
ised by the local government, had a run-down, uncared-for appearance. Seamus was distressed because of the state of the building
and also because he did not meet anyone that he knew so he said to
Tommy Murphy, 'Let's forget about going to Nanfeng. I am tired of
seeing empty desolate churches.' So they drove back to Nancheng.
Still, although there were a lot of depressing features, he also found
the visit informative and inspiring.

Jim Yang, although he was unable to see Seamus, sent him a message, part of it like the letter Jim sent to us in 1980, re-affirming his
loyalty to the Pope, part of it saying that he, Jim, 'has many followers
around Nancheng'. My understanding of that sentence is that very
many Catholics of the diocese have got in touch with Jim since he
came back to Nancheng or sent him messages of their continual
loyalty to the Pope as members of the Roman Catholic Church. Jim
died on the 29th November 1988, a few weeks after Seamus left
China. Fr Peter Hsieh performed the burial rite which was private
and simple as the authorities did not allow the Catholics to have a
public funeral. As I think of Jim now, words from the 'Pilgrim's
Progress' seem apt: 'So he passed over and all the trumpets sounded
for him on the other side.'

Seamus's visit encouraged me to write to Tommy Yu for Christmas
the next year, 1989. In reply, Tommy says 'many thanks for your
letter and your beautiful Christmas card; it is an unthinkable joy
that after thirty-five years, I can still read your letter and receive
your Christmas card. When my fourth imprisonment was be-
stowed by the Communist Party, I thought I would die in the jail or
in the labour camp, but God has his own way of letting me out. I

am able to do a little bit of work for the poor Chinese people and for his greater glory. All through the years, you have said Mass and prayed for me and my sister, Mi Fwng, and for the Kiutu people. Thanks a lot. I translated your letter into Chinese and sent it to our village where the Catholics of Kiutu will hear it.' In a letter to Seamus O'Reilly, Sr Teresita Yu tells of the Feast of the Assumption in Nancheng this year, 1990. She says, 'Tommy went to Pakan to visit my sister and the relatives. On the 15th August, Our Lady's Feast, he said Mass in Bishop Cleary's Cathedral. There were almost five hundred Catholics present, all of them were very happy. After Mass they had strings of fire crackers.'

On the 22nd September, I received from Teresita Yu the following letter: 'My brother Thomas has been sent to Nancheng Cathedral as parish priest. Fr Peter Hsieh will come down from Yingtan on the feast of the Holy Rosary and they will concelebrate Mass that day to thank God. Do you remember the Cathedral is called Holy Rosary Church? Our Lady of the Holy Rosary is patroness of Nancheng diocese.

He himself has no place to stay. Perhaps he'll rent a small room. He asked for prayers to support him that he will continue the mission that the Columbans have left. I would say he will find it very hard as the Patriotic Church authorities watch him. Many of the good old Catholics have gone to God and there will be a shortage of finance.'

When we old Nancheng hands here in Dalgan got this most joyful news, we started a novena of Masses in honour of Our Lady of the Holy Rosary and we had a 'whip around' and sent a few bob to Sr Teresita for Tommy.

Less than two weeks later, I had another letter from Sr Teresita Yu, written on 21st October. The letter informed me that the Feast of the Holy Rosary was celebrated in Nancheng Cathedral with great joy and that hundreds of people attended the Mass. Our two surviving Chinese priests, Fr Tommy Yu and Peter Hsieh, concelebrated. She says that now that the Catholics know that Tommy Yu is the parish priest of Nancheng, many are coming for Sunday Mass from different villages. In the evening, he goes to the families to say the rosary with them. He says that he is very happy.

So maybe this is the happy ending for which Fr Sigsmund was frantically searching in his sermon. Hopefully, and with the help of your prayers, this is the happy ending of my Nancheng story. I can hear Bishop Cleary say to me, 'Did you notice that the first public Mass since 1952 was said in the Cathedral of the Feast of the Assumption, 1990, and that Tommy Yu set out on his journey to Nancheng on the 8th September, Birthday of Our Lady, and that you received so much good news during the month of the Holy Rosary, October?' Since the Red take-over, he always looked towards Our Blessed Lady, especially on her big feasts, to show us some sign of her maternal love and to help us to read the signs of the times. Seamus and I can now testify that he was never disappointed in his hopes and that in all these days she was Our Lady of Perpetual Help because she is our Beloved Mother. She is our Lady of Sorrows and she stood beside our Chinese priests during their long, bitter years of sorrow, pain and trial, just as she stood beside the cross. But she is also Our Lady of Transitions, of happy endings and new beginnings. Above all, she is the cause of our joy.

For us Columbans whom you have met in this story, the evening of life has already come. But you have to wait till the evening to see what a wonderful day it has been. We are full of gratitude for the supreme joy of being priests and of being called to witness and shepherd our people in persecution. We are also most grateful to God for the outstanding co-missionaries the good God has sent us. This story is dedicated to them. I have had the privilege of meeting them after Masses at which I have preached in very many parishes in England, Scotland and Ireland. I saw pensioners stint themselves to help us materially. More importantly, I have seen them come to me enthusiastically offering their prayers, their pain, their sickness for our Chinese Catholics and priests in Nancheng and for all our missions. In the schools I have visited I found the same kind of enthusiasm, amongst the sisters, brothers, teachers and pupils.

Sir James Barrie, the Scottish playwright has said, 'They who bring sunshine into the lives of others cannot keep it from themselves.' May the sunshine of God's love and hope and joy, which our co-missionaries have helped us to bring into the lives of other people, be reflected back into their own lives and stay with them through the passage of the years.